To
Arlene Layman
from Carol
with best wishes

`D1548499`

Growing Up Rich in Vernon, Indiana

A celebration of
American small-town life in the 1940s and '50s

by Carol Spurlock Layman

Still Waters Press

North Vernon   Indiana 47265

For information contact **Still Waters Press**, 2730 W CR 200 N, North Vernon, Indiana 47265. Phone (812) 346-2780.

10 9 8 7 6 5 4 3 2

Publisher's Cataloging in Publication Data
Layman, Carol Spurlock
Growing up Rich in Vernon, Indiana: A celebration of American
      small-town life in the 1940s and '50s
Includes index
1. Vernon (Ind.) - Social Life and Customs, 1940-1950 - Anecdotes
2. Vernon (Ind.) - Anecdotes
3. Layman, Carol Spurlock - Biography
4. Indiana, Southeastern - Anecdotes
           977.217
ISBN 0-9631855-7-8: $19.95 Hardcover
Library of Congress Catalog Card Number: 92-80229

Printed and bound in the United States of America
Smyth sewn, acid-free paper

ACKNOWLEDGMENTS

I will forever appreciate the contributions, in the form of shared photos, memories, and advice, provided by the Cadby and Layman families and by the following Vernonites:

Pete Adamaitis, David Alexander, Bill Arthur, Ben Barber, Jr., Mary Grinstead Barber, Ted Bennett, Lucille Bolser, Ruth Calvert Boswell, Tom Bowerly, Karen Boggs Branham, Kay Boggs Brown, Mildred Brown, Charles Cartwright, Lethia Cartwright, Norman Cartwright, Vernon Cartwright, Florence Collins, Marilyn Fry Collins, Sue Armstrong Collins, Ted Collins, J. W. Coombs, Joe Coombs, Alice Roberson Coombs, Christine Walt Costelow, Mary Lee Cull, Shirley Dawson, Wilford Day, Mary Lou Patterson Duff, Betty Whiteaker Dugan, Rose Simpson Eder, Faye Engle Ellis, Carol Kingen Engle, Ruth Engle Estes, Virginia Tull Estlick, Stella Fisher, Hazel Sandefur Flack, Wilson Flack, Peggy Summerfield Fording, Bob Fry, Patrick Fry, Marjorie Stewart Funke, Norman Griessbach, Susie Rogers Hall, Ida Fisher Harding, Steve Harding, Elaine Roseberry Hart, Charles Hartwell, Rozanna Hartwell, Bob Heaton, Joyce Bowerly Hubbard, Mary Hulse, Cab Hunt, Gilbert Hunt, Bo Ingram, Charles Ingram, Margaret Cartwright Jackson, Ben Johnson, Frances Fawcett Johnson, Fred Johnson, Matle Cartwright Johnson, Naomi Johnson, Mary Wolfinger Jolly, John Jones, Ralph Jordan, Charles Kirkham, Opal Kirkham, Virginia Bowerly Lucas, Barbara Patterson McCoy, Joyce Whitcomb McKeand, Alberta Marsh, Evelyn Mathews, Hellen Ochs, Rosanna Sandefur Oldham, Cynthia Crist O'Mara, Mary Crist Pace, John Patterson, Bill Powell, Mary Roberson Proctor, Norma Stearns Redmond, Margaret Reese, Mark Rieser, Albert Roberson, Edna Roberson, John Roberson, Tom Roberson, Eddie Rogers, Mike Rogers, Wayne Rogers, Jim Sallee, Norma Sallee, Lena Sampson, Forrest Sandefur, Mayme Sandefur, Chester Sanders, Florence Sanders, Paul Sandlin, Lorena Schnadinger, Ethel Scott, Doris Shaw, Bob Shaw, Marjorie Fry Shinolt, Florence Simpson, Eleanor Skinner, Zola Slone, Juanita Fitch Speer, Marie Jones Speer, Treva Hughey Stark, Helen Walt Taylor, Ruth Grant Triana, Ada Keuthan Trowbridge, Marilyn Arney Tungeitt, Bernice Keuthan Wessel, Eulalee Smith White, Don Whiteaker, Betty Williams, Betty Willman, Dick Willman, Betty Bennett Wilson, and Lawrence Wolfinger.

Thanks also go to these individuals for their contributions: Ilah and Larry Allsop, Richard Andrew, Kathleen Berry, Lillian Carmer, Jody Ebinger, Tim Evans, Margaret Flowers, Nancy Edmonds Hanson, John Kocur, John Losey, Kerri McIntire, Patrick Morley, Lura Bennett Shannon, Mary Lynn Whitcomb, and Laura Adamaitis Williams.

I wonder if the crimson oaks will ever look so fine, burn with such inward fire, and toned with such an envelope of ashen gray as those we used to see at Vernon. Somehow the things at Vernon seem to be the standard by which things are judged.

T.C. Steele, 1895

CONTENTS

IF WHAT THEY SAY IS TRUE, that it takes a village to raise a child, then my contemporaries and I were reared by the little Indiana town of Vernon, as it was in the 1940s and '50s.

It was Vernon who taught us that the unwashed were to be given a seat at the table, the homeless a regular berth, and the cantankerous a wide berth.

On a typical day we could inspect a newborn baby, then cross the street to a front porch and visit with an old person. We came to know a lot about babies and old people, but our most valuable lessons came in witnessing the process whereby humans move along between those two poles.

We didn't know some of our fellow Vernonites soon enough, some we didn't know well enough, and some we didn't know long enough. But, as for me, I gladly accept every one of them as being part of my parentage, even Skyline Bill, the Old Dutch Cleanser Women, Little Ploog, and Jake Swarthout, the grouchiest man in town.

I want to tell you about that Vernon of the '40s and '50s, but I can't. I'm an adult, and we adults find ourselves mincing a word here, varnishing a word there, until we've squeezed the very spirit right out of the story.

So I'm relinquishing the narration to a plainspoken girl named Carol Jeanette. She can better describe the people, places, and events of her town, and she'll begin by introducing you to...

JAKE SWARTHOUT

Some grown-ups said Jake Swarthout had a good streak in him. They told us about how he used to give Vernon boys jobs in the flour mill, and take them on selling trips through Kentucky. They said he'd instruct one of his men to drive Old Johnny Jones to his dirt-floor house in the country in bad weather, or to "Take my car and deliver those church ladies to their missionary meeting." He was known to weigh kids on the big mill scales and let them ride on the dollies the men used for moving bags of flour.

By the time my generation came along, though, that good streak in Jake Swarthout had narrowed down to just about nothing. To us he was the man who invented new uses for the walking cane. For one thing, it was an educational tool. When we wanted to remember the word "radius" we just thought of Jake Swarthout's cane, and how it formed a circle we didn't dare enter.

Even though he wasn't the music director in the Vernon Baptist Church, he used it to direct the music. Sitting in the aisle in his captain's chair with a flowered pillow on the seat, he'd startle everybody out of their shoes by whacking that cane down on a pew back, right in the middle of a hymn. "We can sing better than this!" he'd bellow. Sometimes he even spit on the sanctuary floor.

JAKE SWARTHOUT
AND CANE

Believe it or not, Jake had girlfriends, mostly out of town, but he went with a Vernon widow for several years. He must have really liked her because he bought her a ballpoint pen for Christmas. Jake usually broke up with his girlfriends in December so he wouldn't have to buy them presents.

11

One day he painted his cane white, when it seemed he could see what was going on two blocks away. From then on he would swing that cane straight up at the highway, throw his head back, and start across without looking either way. People who couldn't even see what was going on would hear semi brakes hissing and car tires squealing and comment to one another, "Jake's crossing the highway."

When waiting semi drivers rolled their windows down and told Jake he'd better be careful, he'd snap back, "I was here before this highway!" If a semi didn't get stopped soon enough and Jake had to walk around any part it, he ran his cane along the side until he got to the end, just to remind the driver for his next trip through Vernon.

Jake fought with everybody, even his neighbor ladies. When Mrs. Welker was his neighbor, before she was his landlady, he fought with her over the property line and she hit him with a skillet. Jake hit Eva Jordan with a hoe for the same reason. Some Vernon kids who went to investigate the incident said they found blood on the ground. Janie Rogers asked him to quit emptying his pot in the enclosed alley between their homes, and he *threw the contents on her.*

He punched our preacher. "Right in the vestibule," I heard somebody say. I didn't know what part of a man's body that was and I didn't ask. The preacher's wife was standing there holding the white gloves she sometimes used to signal her husband that his sermon was running too long. Before the church people could get the three separated, she slapped Jake with those gloves and he slapped her with his bare hand!

Jake moved around among Vernon's three churches because he would get mad at a church or a church would ask him to leave. We heard stories of his causing trouble in the Presbyterian church, too, by yelling at the preacher, "Well, I can't hear ya!"

In Hunt's store he would stand right in the middle of the aisle and make people walk around him. He thought he owned other buildings, too. He once stirred up the whole town by threatening to cut down one of the spirea bushes at the side of the courthouse. He said it rubbed against him and got dew on his coat when he started into the building on his daily rounds through the offices, probably to check on the Republicans. Whenever he met a Republican, he'd say, "There are two kinds of Republicans—bad and dead. If you're living, you know what you are."

After Henry Hulse opened Vernon's first laundromat in the building behind the post office, Jake started throwing his dirty clothes into a washer with somebody else's to get out of paying. Then he had the nerve to accuse Mr. Hulse of stealing one of his sheets. Kids eating ice cream cones stayed away from him because he'd grab their cones and give them nickels, just so he wouldn't have to walk to the drugstore. Sometimes he didn't even give the nickel.

Jake boarded at Welker's house, one of the brick row houses facing the highway and the courtyard. There were two front doors and his was on the right. The porch, the only one on the block, was high off the sidewalk and reminded me of the end of a caboose, as if a train had run into the house and the end of the caboose was all that was sticking out. It needed to be draped in red, white, and blue bunting and have a politician waving at the people. Instead, Jake sat up there on a padded glider with a big cigar sticking out of the middle of his mouth, looking like the president of the world.

My sister Katie and I, when about half-grown, made a discovery—Jake Swarthout and Harriet McKinney were brother and sister! Here they lived on the same block, only a few houses apart, and never spoke to each other. Jake told Mrs. Welker's granddaughters, the Boggs twins, that Harriet McKinney was a witch. "You shouldn't skate near her place," he said. But they did anyway and ended up liking her. And instead of putting them in her oven, she gave them some of those clay marbles she made that weren't perfectly round. The twins took the marbles back to their grandmother's house and Jake played marbles with them, while they tried to talk him into making up with his sister.

Mrs. Welker was our church pianist and sometimes, to prevent heating up the church for just a few hours, we practiced the Christmas program at her house in groups. We stood in a semi-circle around her piano, singing our songs about peace on earth and good will toward men while twisting our heads around to sneak a look at Jake's room. It was always dark, like a cave. Craning our necks in the other direction, toward the kitchen, we tried to see the little berry bowl Mrs. Welker served his stewed raisins in every day.

Jake's bed was right up against the front window. Kids who got to stay out after nine P.M. said if you walked past that window on a summer night, you could see him lying against the screen with his eyes open. We didn't know if he slept with his eyes open or just opened them when he heard footsteps on the sidewalk.

After Mr. Welker died and Mrs. Welker moved to the big house her family owned across the highway from us, Jake bought the row house and continued to live there. But he no longer had a cook and housekeeper, so he tried to pull off about the most brazen thing he ever did, which *really* made Mrs. Welker mad.

Jake Swarthout, who had never been married, walked over to the clerk's office and said he wanted a marriage license. "Who are you going to marry?" the clerk asked.

"Mrs. Welker," Jake answered.

"Where is she?" the clerk asked. "She'll have to sign, too."

"I haven't told her yet," Jake said.

THINGS YOU MIGHT NOT KNOW ABOUT VERNON

The Creation of Vernon

After God had finished making the earth and had rested, he was struck by an impulse to sprinkle extra-special spots all over the globe. Obeying this impulse, he chose for one of these an area that would later be called the United States of America, narrowing the site down to a state that would be called "Indiana" and a county that would be named "Jennings" after Indiana's first governor.

Holding his finger to his lips, God studied this place he had chosen. It was completely flat—and muddy, of course, as the earth was brand new and not yet dry. "This spot is just too special to be run over by the masses," he thought, "or to sprawl out of control. I'll fix it so only about 500 people can live here at any one time."

God stuck his forefinger in the mud at the northwestern corner of this special place and started to etch a perfect circle around it. But he stopped and shook his head, patted down the mud, and began again. This time, with a twinkle in his eye, he etched a *wavy* line, all the way around the special place.

Clear water rushed into this trench, the leading wave closely following God's finger. Right behind this crest catfish and goggle-eye checked out the river bottom while bluegill and crappie jumped playfully into the air, almost touching the butterflies trying their wings overhead.

By the time God returned to the spot where he had begun, a big pile of mud was pushed up in front of his finger. Being a loving God, he left some of it right there, providing a razorback land-crossing for the people. "I'll give them *one* place to cross the river without getting their feet wet," he said. But a lot of mud was left over, and with it having been sanctified, he couldn't take it out of the circle.

At first God didn't know what to do with the leftover clay, then he said, "I *am* a loving God; I don't want these

15

people living in a mud hole." He started mounding up the clay in the middle of the circle. "I'm also a just God, so I'll make this a high mountain and let them earn the privilege of living here."

In the end God's loving side won out over his just side. He took some of the mud off the top and shaped the hill into a rounded ridge that sloped down to the river on both sides and each end. With the soil he had removed, he made a smaller ridge on the south side of the main ridge, right at the narrowest part of the hourglass. (The town ended up being shaped similar to an hourglass, with one end for the living and one end for the dead.)

"They'll name this place 'Vernon' after the home of their first president," he said, talking to himself while he worked. "It'll be the county seat, so we'd better leave a level area for the courthouse." When he was finished, God looked down on this special place that would be Vernon and he said, "It is good."

John Vawter Plants a Town

Now God had intended to let Adam and Eve live in Vernon, after trial runs in lesser places, but when he saw how they botched up their very first location, he reconsidered and kept Vernon to himself, sort of a home-away-from-home. It was many years later, along about Genesis Eleven, when God scattered Adam and Eve's descendants all over the earth and gave them different tongues and different shades of skin, that he directed the tawny-colored people toward Vernon. When they found it, they loved it dearly and named the river Muscatatuck, but later they were forced to move northward and the place once again became a secret.

Not long after that, when the War of 1812 had ended, a United States surveyor named John Vawter happened upon the special spot. Not believing his eyes, he said to himself, "What a perfect place for a town called Vernon."

16

John Vawter bought a square mile that included this jewel and the setting around it. Then he rode back down to the Ohio River town of Madison, gathered up his family, and returned. At the corner of the special place where the south fork enters the river, he built a two-room cabin of logs.

In late 1815, sitting beside a flickering candle in his new house, he put the finishing touches on his plan for Vernon. "Come look at this, Polly," he said to his wife. Polly, carrying their baby Emily in her arms, came over to the table. Looking down at the parchment map, she saw about two dozen whole blocks and various perimeter pieces whose shapes were determined by the meandering of the Muscatatuck. The river was allowed to keep its name, by the way, which, according to the most popular legend, means "Winding Waters."

"I'm giving a third of the lots to the people," John Vawter said, "and ten percent of the sales from the others will be set aside for a free county library. It'll be the first one in the United States." He showed Polly all the places for schools and churches. "And here is where we'll put the seat of government." He pointed to the exact place God had prepared.

Then he arose and walked over to a window. "And right out there—you know what it looks like in the daylight—that grassy area the river curves around—we'll set it aside for a common ground that will always belong to the people." This public area, the first in Indiana, became known as "The Commons" about the same time the land-crossing on the upper end of town became known as "The Narries," spelled N-A-R-R-O-W-S.

By the spring of 1816 there were enough settlers in the Vernon area that John Vawter and six other persons could draw up eleven "rules of decorum" and establish a Baptist church. This group, being "sensible of the advantages of church privileges," met at various places until they erected a square brick building on the east end of the main ridge.

17

Some years later, in the late 1830s, when John Vawter was taking an evening stroll around Vernon, he paused in front of this church in which he often preached. Standing on this high point, without benefit of compass or chain, he surveyed his town, directing his gaze slowly from east to west, from the Commons to the Narries. When he had finished taking stock of the Vernon that lay below him, he raised his arms high into the air and shouted, "It is good!"

The Stork Stops at Vernon

Was my getting to grow up in Vernon an act of God? or was this where the stork happened to be when his wings became waterlogged from January rains that made the Ohio River rage toward her worst flood in recorded history?

My daddy, Dick Spurlock, wanted me to be a son born on his birthday, but in my first and last really defiant act toward him, I held off until just after midnight and came out as a girl. He probably wasn't too upset, though. He didn't know then that my mother, Virginia, would present him with a total of *five* girls before any sons were born and that his friends would be calling him "Eddie Cantor Spurlock," or tease him because he could remember the birth dates of his hunting dogs but not his children.

They had lost their first daughter, Betty Evelyn, when she was nine months old, so that left their second daughter, Dorothy, who was two and a half, to be the only sibling to greet me when I came into the world.

The Vernon I entered had grown and ungrown in the hundred years since John Vawter stood on the hill and admired his town. For starters, the Baptist Church building he stood in front of had been replaced in 1871 with a longer, wider one, also made of brick and topped with a tall steeple on the front.

There was a hollow metal ball on the very tip of this steeple and woodpeckers liked to make an awful racket on that thing when trying to get the attention of their girlfriends, usually before daybreak. By the time I married Don Layman in this church in 1956, the hollow metal ball was gone and I didn't know what had happened to it. I thought somebody probably shot it off the steeple at 4:30 one summer morning and threw it at a woodpecker.

Nevertheless, if John Vawter had stood here in front of this church after one hundred years, he would have seen evidence of powerful men messing with his plan for Vernon. For one thing, they had brought State Road 3 through town in the early 1930s. This was a real, cement highway, not like SR7, which was already there but didn't really show, and just kind of found its way through town and across a long, steel bridge. The new bridge was made of cement and was held up by five arches. There was a popular song written about it, called, "Underneath the Arches."

State Road 3 changed the town a little bit, but the powerful men had been careful to do as little damage as possible. Instead of cutting directly through the town, which would have divided half the squares diagonally, they created three curves, just nipping off the corners of a few blocks.

A couple of houses were removed to make way for the north curve, and for the south curve my grandpa, C. C. Cadby, had to rebuild his grocery store. When the Rogers house was moved back for the middle curve, Josie Rogers was pretty upset. She had a highway cutting through her front yard and her catalpa tree was sitting in a little triangle way across on the other side. From then on, they say, she guarded that tree like it was one of her children.

So now, in addition to her Commons and her Narries, Vernon had what was called the "Y," where State Roads 3 and 7 parted company south of town on the other side of the river.

Progressively-minded John Vawter probably would have liked the highway. And even if he didn't like it, it served him right. He had messed with *God's* plan for Vernon. In 1837 he and some other powerful men built a *third* ridge in the town, for a railroad track.

From the Narries end of town this steep ridge rose up to fifty feet and continued at that height until meeting a trestle that crossed the river at the Commons. Everybody felt sorry for John New when the surveyors' stakes came within twenty feet of his nice house at the corner of Pike and Gaines. Now, instead of gazing on the Muscatatuck below, he would be staring at a dirt wall and one end of a limestone arch that would soon be known as the "culvert."

So naturally the opponents of this Madison-to-Vernon railroad, knowing they were losing the battle, laughed out loud when the surveyors ran their line right through John Vawter's front hall. But John Vawter, anxious to have the first elevated track in Indiana and the first underpass in the United States, wasn't bothered by that. He simply moved his house across the street and didn't say a word when his garden and orchard were covered by the embankment.

God finally did have to put his foot down though, when he saw that too many people could crowd into Vernon, that more than a thousand people had lived there in the 1850s when construction on the courthouse was begun. He didn't want that to happen again, so he sent two tornadoes through the town.

The first one, in 1917, was just a warning tornado. The second one, in 1932, was a bad one. No people were killed, but a lot of two story brick buildings became one story buildings, and a few had to be torn down. And Vernon's population remained just above 400 from then on.

Actually, God didn't need to do this. He had already accomplished it when he laid out the setting for Vernon, because even though the Madison railroad was later continued

Left: THE CEMENT BRIDGE WHEN NEW; OLD BRIDGE IN BACKGROUND

21

to Indianapolis, there was room for only one railroad track in our town. So when the O & M came through southern Indiana about the time the courthouse was finished, it crossed our track two miles to the north and most of Vernon's 100 merchants moved up there. Other railroads intersected at that point and soon the new town to the north was larger than Vernon.

When I came into the picture, Vernon was in the last stages of being self-contained. If you were reasonably healthy and kept your money under your mattress, you could live your entire life without ever crossing the river or the Narries. Then, after a three-day layover at Jordan's Funeral Home, your body would be taken to the other end of the hourglass where it would spend eternity.

But I don't know of anyone who did it that way. Vernonites went to North Vernon for lots of reasons. The main one for us kids was a once-a-year event called the county fair, held in North Vernon's city park under three dozen giant oak trees. It was here one summer, when I was half-grown, that I realized how Vernon operated.

I was looking down at a miniature wooden village somebody had fixed up. This little town was full of hand-carved mechanical people about two inches tall, all doing things and grouped together according to their jobs. In the timbering section, my favorites were the two fellows using a crosscut saw. In the housekeeping section I liked the woman raising and lowering a bucket into a well. Each little person or pair worked at its own rhythm.

Stepping back one step I could see how the individual movements contributed to the rhythm of each section, and each section added to an overall rhythm of the entire village. Then it hit me. "Hey!" I said aloud, "this is *Vernon*."

A couple of people looked at me funny and I quickly moved back to the security of the little village. Staring at it in this new light, I was filled with a sense of satisfaction and whispered to myself, "It is good."

THE RHYTHMS OF VERNON

The Spurlock Household

At first I knew only the rhythms of the Spurlock household, and I wasn't old enough to notice them until we had moved across the highway, to an apartment above my grandpa's store on the inside of the south curve. By that time I had a little sister called "Katie," who was born when I was fourteen months old and still too fat to walk.

Looking at the store building, a lot of people thought the front of the Sandford Tavern, which had been the home of Jennings County's first merchant, had been cut off at an angle when the highway came through, but that wasn't true. Using some of the material out of the old store, and anything else he could scrounge up, Grandpa had built his new store in this shape deliberately. The part we lived over was my uncle Lloyd's filling station, a place called "Shotgun's."

We called our apartment our "house." It was separated into three rooms by partitions that didn't go all the way to the ceiling. Each room was so big it required two linoleums, sometimes of two different patterns, which made perfect roads for little cars and trucks. Our "front" door was actually at the back and side of the building, where the upstairs part touched the ground. When entering, you were in what we called our "front room." The partition wall here was varnished car siding and it was the most beautiful wall in Vernon.

To the left of the front door, under two high windows whose not being the same shape was hidden by our mother's sewing skills, was what we called the "waterent table." Grandpa had made it. He made everything out of oak and made it to last for centuries, so the waterent table was very heavy. This was where our mother did her paperwork when she was the town clerk-treasurer and people came to our house to pay their water rent. Most of the time, though, it was covered with our own projects.

23

The "hospital scissors" usually were lying on the waterent table. They were bent in the middle and had a round, flat thing on the tip of the longest blade. Our aunt Betty, who was a nurse, had left them for us because they were safe. She said they were for cutting off bandages.

On the other side of the front room was our daddy's chair, his floor lamp, floor ashtray, the table radio, and a wood and coal stove that was our only source of heat. Our couch was in front of the car siding, and our daddy's upright piano was against the end wall.

In front of the piano was our one nice piece of furniture—a shiny piano bench. This bench was to be avoided in any game of "poisent floor," a game in which we had to travel about the room on furniture because the floor was poison. A shoe print found on this bench could bring about a lineup. When that happened, you hoped the print didn't match your shoe, which could bring about a whack with a yardstick. We soon discovered we could play poisent floor in our socks, but it was still against the rules.

Half of the partition wall was set out in front of the other so the doorway to the bedroom where we all slept didn't need a curtain on it. Since the bedroom was between the front room and the kitchen, we had to walk through it all the time. We each had a shelf in this room for our toys and other valuables.

The bedroom and the kitchen were separated by a wide partition full of shelves on the kitchen side. In the open space above it was white lattice work covered with vines and that's what the kitchen wallpaper pattern was, white lattice work covered with vines. In the pointed corner of the kitchen our cold water pipe came up through the floor and stood there looking dumb, with a spigot for a head. The "slop bucket" sat beneath it to catch drips and other things. Nearby we had a wash pan on a washstand, and beside that a water bucket with a dipper in it. We all drank out of this dipper, so anybody who accidentally got it down into the wash pan water got yelled at.

Slate, instead of grass, was outside our front door. Maybe this was why we crossed the highway to the courtyard or the funeral home whenever our mother got the camera out. Jimmy Walker, an older boy, once laughed at me when I ordered him out of our yard. "You call this a yard?" he said. "There's not a blade of grass in it."

I started to say, "Well, a stockyard is a yard; a junk yard is a yard," but I didn't like the sound of that. Then I almost said, "For your information, there's gold in this slate; I have some in my treasure box right now," but I didn't want Jimmy Walker to start looking for our gold. So I just stuck my tongue out at him.

ME, DOROTHY, MARY LOU, AND KATIE ON A COURTYARD BENCH
(Mary Lou and Katie wouldn't sit right)

In the early years here I slept through the first steps in the daily rhythm of our family. I never heard Vernon roosters crow or the *Indianapolis Star* thump against the front door. I never heard my mother get up at five-thirty and start a fire so the house would be warm when Daddy got up at six to eat breakfast. I wasn't aware of her own breakfast and coffee while reading the paper in the time between Daddy's leaving for the swing factory and Dorothy's getting up for school.

By the time Mary Lou was born, Katie and I, still pre-schoolers, were as inseparable as a pair of coat hangers. While we played all day, our mother never stopped working. She washed and sewed and cooked and changed Mary Lou's diapers and took people's water rent. She carried out the slop bucket and carried in the coal bucket. But her most important job was having supper ready at four, when the last swing factory whistle blew. Daddy had to eat as soon as he got home so he would have an uninterrupted evening to fish or hunt or play cards. This was how it was with Daddies because they *worked*.

In the evening Mommy did the dishes and emptied the slop bucket again and got us ready for bed. If it was Monday evening, she sprinkled the clothes because she'd washed that day in the back room of the store. On Tuesday evenings she ironed. Sometimes Daddy called her from the kitchen to the front room whenever the stove needed another chunk of coal or wood. Other women got after her for "spoiling" him, but she never complained. She just said she'd rather put the wood in the stove than clean up after he did it.

Saturday nights the kitchen was full of the Saturday night smell, a combination of Ivory suds in a galvanized tub, white shoe polish, Drene shampoo, steaming red Jello, and the insides of a chicken. Freshly washed hair ribbons were wrapped around a glass jar, being dried and ironed at the same time, and a fine-tooth comb waited for the soaking baby. Watching our mother clean the chicken was our Saturday night entertainment. One night when I saw her pull the insides out of the chicken I said, "So *that's* where we get our beans and macaroni!"

This was all in preparation for Sunday, when we walked up the hill with our mother to the Baptist Church for Sunday School. Afterwards, while she fried that chicken, mashed potatoes, and made gravy, we looked at the funny papers and cut out Dixie Dugan paper dolls. On Sunday evenings, after we had our red Jello for dessert, we all sat around the radio.

Daddy often played the piano at night. He usually played by ear and when he played "Sunrise Serenade" he sounded just like his idol, Frankie Carle. Sometimes, especially when his music-playing friends came in on Saturday night, he played his banjo, which had Christmas lights inside it that lit up and glowed through the skin on the top. He could play his banjo so fast his fingers were just blurs, but on weeknights when we were supposed to be getting settled down for bed, he played quieter songs on the piano.

Once in bed, we girls would lie on our backs and watch headlight beams run across the ceiling, chasing each other in one window and out the other, then back again. This was when the rhythm of *sounds* became noticeable—big trucks coming off the cement bridge shifting gears for the curve. This was when the squeak of the rocking chair in the front room or the swing chain outside always put us to sleep before the baby.

Right after a rain, when the windows were open, was the best time for going to sleep. Every vehicle that crossed the bridge swished four times, where water gathered at the drains between the arches:

swish...swish...swish...swish

On these rainy nights, when sound carried so well, we could hear the locomotive whistle blowing for the Grayford crossing, well before it reached the south fork trestle. And when Billy Powell came through town on his BSA—we knew he was leaning *way* over on the curve—we not only heard his motorcycle roar across the bridge, but we could hear it echo through State Road 7's rocky corridor on beyond the "Y."

The South Curve Neighborhood

As soon as I was able to climb onto the waterent table and look out the window, I graduated from the rhythms of the Spurlock household to the rhythms of the south curve neighborhood   The first person I saw every morning was Harriet McKinney. She would come out her back door with her pot and shuffle up the garden path, reverently carrying the previous night's offerings to a god that looked a lot like an outhouse.

Our neighborhood was busy that time of day. People came to work at the courthouse, delivery trucks stopped at the store, and school buses whizzed past on the highway. Then Dorothy would start up the hill with her lunch sack in her hand. I hated to see her leave and would be back up on that table when it was time for her to come home. After she'd been in school awhile she told us other kids couldn't just look at an object and draw it like she could. I think this surprised her.

Though it would have seemed natural, the activity outside that window didn't come to a standstill while Dorothy was gone. Elaine Heilman would have to come down the hill swinging a two-gallon kerosene can. Pretty soon she would carry it back up the hill, but she wouldn't be swinging it anymore.

Later in the morning Mrs. Welker could be counted on to come down the corner steps carrying a basket with a cloth over it. The cloth was checkered, faded red and white. "What's in Mrs. Welker's basket?" I asked my mother one day. She said the basket was full of warm pies for her husband's restaurant on the other side of our store. Mrs. Welker baked then on a wood-burning cookstove.

Even when she was on her way back home and her basket was empty, Mrs. Welker held onto Nellie Stout's wall while she climbed the steps because one of her legs was bad. She moved slowly and was barely out of sight when high school boys ran down the hill and grown men came toward

Welker's Lunch from all over town. I could tell by looking at their faces they were thinking about Mrs. Welker's warm pies. One man was a lot darker than the others. My mother said his name was Ben Henry.

I didn't know then that Vernon's weekday rhythm was really a cycle of activity hubs that moved about the town in the course of a day. From my window I was witnessing two of them, the courthouse and Welker's Lunch—three, if you count the men coming to play cards at Shotgun's in the evenings. The hubs I couldn't see were the swing factory, the flour mill, the post office, and the school. On Sundays, when the churches were the hubs, I got to participate.

MR. WELKER

The Town

As Katie and I grew older and gradually ventured all over town, we learned the rhythms of other neighborhoods. We got to hear Rosie Arney calling her boys when we visited our cousins up on the other side of the post office. Rosie lived next door in what was called "Rat Row," a long, white frame building with three apartments in it. She called her boys according to their ages, oldest first, and she did it in one breath: "Bob, Bill, Tom, Paul, Pete!"

Thanks to her, everybody could remember the names and order of the Arney boys. Actually, there were only four sons; Pete was a short-legged "RCA Victor" dog that, if not on a leash, was always half a block behind the boys. Rosie changed her voice when she got to Pete's name; she called out his name in a high voice. Rosie Arney protected Pete and her boys. She wouldn't let her boys play at the Commons until they learned to swim. Maybe it was because her first son, Donald, had died before he reached his teens.

29

Women all over town had special ways of calling their kids. Some of them didn't shout at all. Roxana Patterson sang her children's names. Mrs. DeVersey blew a whistle to call her granddaughters. Margaret Adamaitis could whistle through her teeth—without using her fingers—and be heard all over the south end. Then there was Mrs. Cartwright, walking to visit her children who lived in several houses out on State Road 3. She would start making a trilling sound when she got past the "Y" and her grandchildren would hear her and come running.

SOUTH CURVE KIDS — *Seated*: ALLAN JAMES, TOMMY ROBERSON, EDNA ROBERSON, MARY LOU, DENNY JAMES, AND TEDDY IN FRONT OF IDA BELLE FISHER. *Standing*: ME, JOHNNY ROBERSON, KATIE, AND RONNIE LAKE

Something often happened in the north curve neighborhood that I never got to see, but heard about. It happened whenever there was a fire or a wreck—no matter what time of night or day. Tom Semon's wife Flossie, a very proper lady who wore her rouge in perfectly round patches, would come out on her porch in a beautiful flowing gown. I suppose it was some kind of dressing gown. She must have kept them handy so she could throw one on when she heard the sirens, then come out and stand between those white pillars and say, "Where is it? Where's the fire? Where's the wreck?"

GRANDMA AND GRANDPA CADBY

Cadby's Store

The main part of Cadby's Store was one big room, with wide floorboards, shelves all around the sides, and tables and racks in the middle. It was darkish and always smelled like bread—unless Grandma hadn't gone through the fruit recently. At one side was a long counter of wood Grandpa had built. He put the scales on one end and the cash register on the other. In the summer, a spiral or two of fly paper hung down from the ceiling.

The person running the store got to sit behind the counter on a big can that contained the matches and had a flowered pillow on top of it, every bit as nice as Jake's. When you were behind the counter, you could see all the little nooks for sacks, and the books with customers' names on the tops. Our grandpa always said, "Whenever they get a little cash, they go to Hunt's." But we found out that's what Hunt's said about Cadby's...and Shaw's. Sometimes men came in and gave Grandpa their whole paychecks, and still weren't paid up.

Dorothy worked in the store as soon as she was old enough, just as our mother had done when she was a girl. Dorothy got so she knew what people were going to buy before they told her. Mr. Monday, white from head to foot with stone quarry dust—even his eyelashes

KATIE AND THE SPUD GIRL

31

were white—always got two pounds of ginger snaps for his kids. His sister Eugenia Stoner would be white, too, covered with cotton fuzz from the rug factory in North Vernon. Artie Wells walked to our store when he got off at the swing factory, then carried his gunny sack of groceries home to the country. His right shoulder was wider than his left shoulder from carrying that heavy sack for so many years.

We knew all the delivery men. Keith Denton, who delivered gasoline to the station, teased our little brothers without mercy. One of them got so mad he called Keith a

PAULINE CALLON AND
AUNT VONDA ON THE
DR. PEPPER TRUCK

Democrat. Some delivery men came once a week, some twice a week, and some daily, like the bread men.

Clarence "Posey" Barnes was the feistiest bread man in the world, even if he did call little girls "Sweetie" and deliver bread to country houses. He and his pretty wife lived up near the north curve, but never associated with anybody very much. Everyone knew he never picked up Vernon hitchhikers when on his way to North Vernon in his new car, and almost everyone knew he had gone to a council meeting and tried to get the town speed limit changed. "Ten miles an hour is too low," he said very politely. "I've got a new car and I can't get it out of low gear." Nobody else in town had a new car, so Posey didn't get any sympathy.

Once when Roger Barnes and my little brother Teddy were ricocheting fist-sized rocks off the sides of semi trailers coming around our curve, Posey came around in his bread truck and Roger broke his windshield. Posey stopped his truck and chased Roger until he caught him, then gave him a good spanking. Posey told our mother, and she spanked

Teddy with her extra heavy yardstick—the one she used for measuring wallpaper—and broke it in two places.

Posey Barnes delivered bread for several companies, those wide loaves that were heart-shaped on the top. He wasn't too happy when Butternut came out with their long loaves of single slices. That's probably why he did what he did the day he came in and found that a tall loaf of Butternut had fallen over on his Bewley's bread.

He stood that loaf of Butternut on the rack, on end, and hit it with his fist as hard as he could. Dorothy had just started working in the store. "I could barely see over the counter," she said later, "and I know my eyes got big when Posey Barnes did that."

She said they both looked at the loaf of Butternut, which was now only about four inches long. Posey took it out to his truck, brought in his own bread, apologized, and paid for the Butternut.

Grandma and Grandpa Cadby

Like most grandmas, Grandma Cadby always looked worried, kept her gray hair in a topknot, and had trouble finding shoes that wouldn't hurt her bunions. She wore aprons with armholes in them over dresses printed with little bitty flowers and used dish towels made out of flour sacks. Whenever she looked out the store window and saw a man—any man—approaching, she would say, "Now, Clarence, don't get into an argument with him."

Grandpa loved to argue politics and religion. He sometimes played religious music over a loud speaker so everybody in the south end of town could enjoy it. He caused a stir in our church when he bought a new movie projector and started showing religious movies in his yard. Some people thought his goal was to replace preachers with movies.

Grandpa's hat was one of those soft caps with a small bill on it, a touch of England left over from his ancestors.

He wore overalls or pants held up with suspenders, black leather, high top shoes, and eyeglasses from the dime store.

He didn't trust doctors. He said they had a cure for cancer, but kept it to themselves because they wanted to profit from the disease. So when he got a skin cancer in

GRANDPA CADBY STICKING
HIS TUMMY OUT

back of his ear, he used remedies he'd heard about on a Chicago radio station. For awhile he wore pieces of raw bacon hanging over his ear and resting on the cancer. I think the cancer liked the bacon, because it kept growing and he finally went to a doctor and had it removed.

I don't remember his working in the store as much as his stopping in there, to cut a piece of cheese off the big cloth-covered cheddar wheel with his pocketknife, or throw a handful of peanuts into the meat grinder, or give away more candy then he sold. Whenever any woman came into the store early in the day, he would say, "Morning, Glory."

He was always playing jokes on people. When Evelyn Bowerly came into the store with hiccups, he cured them by accusing her of shoplifting. He stopped some boys from stealing his blackberries by painting the berries with tar. But he went too far with his jokes when he wired a bench with 110 electricity and some boys who had just swam at the Commons sat on it. Wilford Day went to the hospital and was sick for a week.

Besides running a print shop, Grandpa always had other projects going. He built things without patterns, using native lumber from a farm he'd bought near Westport. He once built a glass showcase for the filling station and the back glass lacked half an inch of reaching the top of the frame. When Mark Rieser asked him about the open crack, Grandpa said "That's so if flies get in the case, they can go to the top and get out again."

Their House across the Highway

Grandma and Grandpa's house was really old. The brick part of it, built before 1830, had been a tavern back when the intersection of Jackson and Posey Streets was the business district. Grandpa built the wooden part on when he bought it. Our Aunt Vonda said she watched him take the insides out of an old upright piano, shove it into the wall, and call it a closet.

We liked the house's L-shaped front porch edged with a wall of open brickwork just high enough to sit on. The holes between the bricks were good mail boxes, just like the Vernon post office. The longest swing in Vernon hung on this porch, long enough we grandchildren could all sit in it and read the Sunday funnies, except when Grandpa was taking a nap there.

We always had to be careful when playing inside this house. There were tipsy things like overhanging ferns sitting on oak stands. We liked playing Monopoly and other board games at Grandma's because hers didn't have any pieces missing. The cellar was great. It had a dirt floor with boards to walk on, and smelled damp and musty. Coal was kept down there, and shelves of home-canned food draped with cobwebs.

Outside was good for playing tag because of the obstacles—walls of lace stretched on thin, wood frames, shirts and dresses snapping their arms at us from the clothesline, or heavy rugs that just hung there, waiting for somebody to beat them. Grandma also had a round tulip bed in the side yard, a grape arbor, spirea bushes, and all those pointy little plants she called hens and chickens.

She didn't have a separate outhouse. Instead, there was a little room with three holes at the end of the wood-shed. I used to brag about my grandma having a three-hole outhouse, two big ones and a smaller, lower one. I don't know why there were three holes; I never saw a group go in there.

Grandma cooked delicious meals on a big, black wood-burning stove, but even better, she made milk shakes by putting some kind of powdered malt in a silver-colored shaker. She let us have maple syrup mixed with butter, *if* we ate a slice of bread with it.

When I was still very small, my grandpa's dad lived there. He was a thin man who sat on the front porch or in a chair at the window, or in his room beside a huge trunk with a sectioned divider in the top. That trunk contained everything he owned in the world and smelled like the candy he kept in it—pink and white peppermints with xxxx on the top, which we liked, and horehound drops, which we didn't like. Wherever he sat, he would have on a black suit with a vest.

When I was three years old, Great-Grandpa Cadby died and was laid out in his black suit and vest in Grandma's living room. That night the family closed the coffin lid and went to bed. Nobody was scared.

Grandpa sold this house to Ben and Naomi Johnson, who had kids we could play with, so we still got to go over there. Grandpa and Grandma moved into the back of the store while he built a new house on our side of the highway.

Cadby's Folly

Grandpa's biggest project in my lifetime was this three-story barn of a house he built—without any visible plan—about halfway up the hill from us, where we'd had those wonderful winding trails through the horseweeds. As usual, his helpers were men working off their debts at the store. Some of them were awfully inept. For a long time the neighbors called the project "Cadby's Folly." Grandpa finished it, though, and got to live in it a few years before he died in 1951.

Like the house they'd lived in across the highway, this one was full of nooks and crannies. I was a teenager now, though, and had outgrown playing hide-'n'-go-seek with my cousins. My sisters and I were more fascinated with the bathroom, but our mother would let us use it only for special occasions.

The last time for me was on May 27, 1956, and when I walked into Grandma's house with my towel and washcloth, she got that worried look on her face—actually, the creased brow was a permanent part of her by now. She said, "I'm sorry it's raining on your wedding day, Carol," as if it were all her fault.

She probably prayed for a nice day, because when I was walking up the hill to marry Don Layman, the sun came out and all of Vernon sparkled.

◦━◦━◦━◦━◦━◦━◦━◦

Things to Do with Empty Boxes from Stores

Post Toasties boxes are the biggest; three or four kids can get into one, but that's about all they're good for. Narrower, longer boxes make good caskets for play funerals, but that's about all they're good for.

The wooden boxes are what you want. Fruit comes in wooden crates divided into two sections. (We were never as lucky as our mother, who found a live tarantula in a crate of bananas when she was a girl, and made it the Cadby Store pet.) Standing on end these wooden crates make perfect cabinets for that playhouse under the apple tree. You can

37

even fix up a curtain on the front, just like your mother does. Boys like to lay them down and make a two-seater car by putting wheels from somebody's dump on them.

Cigar boxes are made of balsa wood, easy to hammer little nails into, not like those hard oak scraps from the swing factory. After some practice, you can cut a round hole in the lid and nail four brads on each end of the circle. Leave them sticking up halfway so you can stretch rubber bands between them. Then nail a handle on it and you have a guitar.

A cigar box makes a great treasure chest, too, something every kid in Vernon needs. First, wait until your dad is painting something. When he lays the brush down, grab it and paint the box. Aluminum paint is good, gives it a silver look. Glue some sets out of old rings, or other pretty things, on the outside. Hide your treasure box where *nobody* can find it, and always make sure nobody is looking when you bring it out.

☼ ☼ ☼ ☼ ☼

ON A 1920s MILL TRIP TO KENTUCKY, JOE SKINNER
AND DONALD ARNEY SEE A MAN DRIVING A GOAT CART

SHOTGUN'S

The filling station side of Grandpa's store was called "Shotgun's" after our Uncle Lloyd, who ran the place. He got his nickname when he was a boy and requested a shotgun for Christmas. Still too young to pronounce his S's, he said, "I want a hot gun to hoot all the hells out in one hot." That was probably the last time he swore, at least in front of the family. Lloyd was very quiet and bashful and never did get married. He blushed a lot.

Bing Crosby stopped at the station once, to ask directions to the Kentucky Derby, and Lloyd got all excited. Everybody in town was talking about it—not about Bing Crosby stopping, but about Shotgun getting excited.

He was generous,

SHOTGUN

too. People suspected that Willard Hartwell, the one they called "Little Ploog," was getting empty pop bottles stored in the back of the station and selling them to Shotgun's for cigarette money. But Lloyd never did anything about it. Also, he had cigar boxes full of paper money in the back room and everybody in town knew it. "Loans" were taken from this cigar box and never repaid. Lloyd was the only merchant in town who sold candy to the band at cost so they could make a bigger profit at the basketball games.

The station was a popular loafing spot. Out in front was a good place to lean a chair back against the wall and watch traffic. It was a good place for putting rotten potatoes in the highway and watching cars run over them. After Dorothy's friend Margie Fry started working in the station, she and Dorothy were out there most of the time when they weren't waiting on customers. I hung around them sometimes, whether they wanted me to or not.

Once when we were all out there I heard one of my favorite songs starting on the radio inside. It was called, "Red's Boogie," a really

DOROTHY

fast song. I ran in and danced a mean boogie because I thought everybody else was outside. But at the end of the song I saw a Vernon man, Cab Hunt, sitting back in the shadows looking at me like I'd gone crazy. I ran outside and told the older girls, which was a mistake, and I was sure happy to see that song go off the radio for good.

The Card Room

My friend Joyce's mother, Lois Whitcomb, said when she was a Vernon girl in the early 1900s, the men gathered on the courthouse steps on summer evenings and sang. I

LURA BENNETT IN
A STEAMER CHAIR

imagined them serenading their wives who were standing in front of open windows doing the supper dishes. The men didn't do that anymore when Joyce and I were girls. Instead, they came to Shotgun's after supper to play cards, like Dagwood and his friends went to Herb Woodley's garage in the

40

funny papers. The men at Shotgun's played euchre mostly, and pinochle and rum and hearts.

The card room was right under us Spurlocks, but we couldn't hear what was being said down there, just the murmur of men's voices. It was kind of a comforting sound when we kids were going to sleep. Once in awhile they did get loud and we could hear what they were saying, usually bad words, something about somebody trumping somebody's ace. If Daddy was upstairs he would yell down the stairway door and say, "Watch your language down there; I'm trying to raise a bunch of girls up here!" Or, if he was down there, he sometimes yelled up for us to be quiet. "We're trying to play cards down here." I was very embarrassed the day I was alone in the house singing opera and he came upstairs and told me to be quiet.

In the summer, when he wasn't playing cards himself, he would sit outside in his steamer chair at the card room window and look down on the action. The window would be swung back with only screen wire covering the opening. Cigarette and cigar smoke rolled up out of there all evening. It looked blue after dark, showing up only in the sharp-edged streak of light that came out the window with it. High school boys coming to the card room for the first time were initiated by being sent to Wenzel's Hardware for a board stretcher, or a sky hook, or a left-handed monkey wrench.

Daddy wouldn't let us get interested in

SHERMAN KING AND BUTCH DAWSON

41

MARGIE FRY PUMPING GAS

any boy who loafed around the card room. We didn't know whether it was because he knew too much about them, or because they knew too much about him.

It seemed a guy wasn't really a part of the card room crowd until he had a nickname. Daddy's was Bab. There also was a Cookie, a Worm, a Slug, a Cotton, a Cue Ball, a Wimpy, a Big Kid, and a Joe-ola. Sometimes, for whatever reason, everybody had an "ola."

Buzz was short for Buzzard. This was Harold Bowerly, who got his nickname when some of the guys were fishing along the river, moving upstream. Harold bent down and gulped a big drink from the river just before they rounded a bend. Once around the turn, they found a huge buzzard roost that stretched all the way across the water, and they never let Harold forget it.

The card room men were always playing jokes on each other. After Casper Clendenning became the town marshal, some of them moved his car over to the front of the sheriff's office one night. Casper was pretty upset when he went outside and discovered his car missing. When he found it, he said he knew who had moved it, a new state trooper named Robert Pond. Nobody ever told him differently. Joe Lunsford once forgot he had driven to the station and he walked home. All the guys were waiting beside his car when he came back after it.

On Sunday afternoons the card room was quiet. The men would have newspapers spread all over the table instead of cards.

The Television Set

Around 1950 Lloyd bought one of the first television sets to come to Vernon. He mounted it high in a corner at Shotgun's and fixed up rows of backless benches and chairs so Vernon people could come in and watch it. Unlike the free movies that used to be shown in the courtyard, these shows weren't going to be canceled by rain. Soon the station was full of people every night and occasionally there were some rather loud town meetings about which show was going to be watched.

A big crowd was always on hand for Friday night wrestling, even women, like Vail Hartwell sitting there in a cloud of cigarette smoke. Between television matches, the boys would go outside and wrestle on the ground. Wrestling fans liked for Lloyd to be running the station on Friday nights because he stayed open until the wrestling was over. His help, on the other hand, would start turning out the lights at closing time.

The high school girls swooned over Eddie Fisher, Perry Como, and the Pee Wee King band in Louisville, while the little kids watched Kukla, Fran, and Ollie and the mothers liked Dinah Shore, Kate Smith, and Nat King Cole. Whole families would come in to watch "Your Show of Shows," Milton Berle, and Lucille Ball. We always knew who'd be in the audience at which time.

BOBBY FRY ON HIS WAY TO WORK AT ROSSES' DAIRY BAR

Lloyd bought any new gadget to do with television sets. For a while he had a piece of rigid blue plastic over the screen that was supposed to protect our eyes. Then he mounted a big TV magnifying glass filled with alcohol to make the picture bigger. Whenever the set broke down, the whole town was shaken, except those few families who had their own televisions (but whose kids found it more fun to watch TV at Shotgun's, with the crowd).

(*L. to R.*) IRVIN JONES, SHOTGUN, YOUNG JOHNNY JONES, AND JOE LUNSFORD

A Little-Known Fact about Vernon

Clay James, a bodyguard for Abraham Lincoln, spent his retirement years in Vernon, living on a government pension in Rat Row. The grey, curly haired Mr. James told his good friend Mort Cartwright he knew all the actors and actresses at the Ford Theater, including John Wilkes Booth. He said he was not on duty the night Lincoln was shot, but later he saw the body of the man they said was Booth. That body was *not* Booth's, Mr. James said. Haskell Cartwright remembered sitting at the man's feet at the age of ten or twelve and listening to his stories.

SITTING ON THE STAIRWAY

When talking to people outside our family, we always had to explain why we Spurlocks did so much "sitting on the stairway," and how we could see our whole neighborhood while we did it. The stairway from the filling station was a secret passageway that came up to the corner of our kitchen. The hole in the floor was covered with a long wooden box about a yard high. The doorway at the end of the enclosure was a square that adults had to crawl through. When a girl was taking a sponge bath or shaving her legs in the kitchen, she *usually* could hear anyone coming up the stairway in time to grab a towel before that door swung open.

The window seat on top of this enclosure was a smaller wooden box with a padded lid. Our Daddy kept his hunting ammo in here, as well as his slingshot. From this high corner of the building we could see the south curve and that whole end of Vernon. Getting big enough to climb up there by yourself and "sit on the stairway" was a great achievement in our family. The seat was a good place for watching rain, doing school lessons—I used my very first ballpoint pen up there—or for talking to other people in the kitchen while they worked.

Daddy did bad things when he sat on the stairway. He teased people, including Willard "Little Ploog" Hartwell. He even teased Mrs. Welker.

When he saw Willard walking home, he reached into the seat and got out that slingshot he'd made out of a perfect hickory fork and a strip of inner tube. Then he turned around to the shelf behind him and got his can of marbles. Even if Willard was halfway to the Commons, Daddy could make a glass marble land just behind him. Willard always looked all around himself, maybe found the marble and studied the sky, but he never did know where the marbles came from.

To tease Mrs. Welker, Daddy didn't have to open the hinged, wood-framed screen on the window; he just blew his crow caller at her, real fast, over and over. This was after she had moved into the house across the curve from us and was an old woman. Her leg was worse now and she always had to struggle to get out of a car. When Daddy made her look for crows up in her trees at the same time, we were embarrassed. Didn't he know Mrs. Welker was the most important person in the Vernon Baptist Church?

MARILYN ARNEY AT THE NARRIES

OUR NEIGHBORS

Nellie Stout and the Simpsons

Nellie Stout, a widow, was our nearest neighbor and the kindest person in the world. She lived right across the street at the end of the brick row houses facing the highway. Her house was so long—it had once been a hotel—she rented out the end toward Harriet McKinney's.

Nellie was old and frail-looking and her back was humped over. Our mother said she used to be tall, but now she had some kind of bone disease older women got. She still had a job, though, working for Wilbur Beeman, an abstractor. Every day she carried a tiny portable typewriter over to the courthouse, then carried it back home after work, holding it out in front of herself. Her fingers looked cut off and she could type with only the main finger on each hand. My little brother Ted said she had worn off her fingers by typing all her life, but our mother said she had arthritis.

She had a big collection of old stamps and coins she let us play with whenever we wanted to, and a brick shed, an old summer kitchen maybe, that was perfect for a late evening game of "handy over." You had *no way* of knowing if a person on the other side had caught that ball, or which way they were coming around to hit you.

Nellie's barn was probably one of Vernon's first, so old we were afraid to play in it. There seemed to be a law in Indiana that people were not allowed to tear down old barns; they had to let them die natural deaths. Hers was just about dead. The junk inside was all that was holding it up.

Nellie Stout's niece, Florence Simpson, had moved out to the country, where she and her husband, Bill, were raising a family of blue-eyed blonds. They came in to the Presbyterian Church every Sunday. When they brought Nellie home from church, all of them piled out of their blue car and we got to play together for awhile.

NELLIE STOUT AND BOB SIMPSON

Bill Simpson was a big man with a gruff voice. The Presbyterian kids said he sang very deep and loud even though he sang off key. They liked to hear him do those *come, come, comes* when they sang "The Church in the Wildwood." When he was township trustee and in charge of Vernon School, the school teachers practically stood at attention every time Bill and Florence Simpson stopped for a visit.

In 1951 a terrible thing happened. Florence Simpson, who hardly ever drove, came barrelling around the curve, blowing the horn, with the whole family in the car. She pulled in at the funeral home. Pretty soon the ambulance left. That night Bobby came over and told me his dad was opening up a wheat field and got his arm caught in a combine and his arm was amputated at the Seymour hospital. While he was telling me about it, I almost fainted.

Rosie and Joan Simpson, both a little older than Dorothy, had been living with Nellie for some time now and Dorothy was very thick with them. Sometimes those big girls disgusted me, though, the way they were always talking in low murmurs I couldn't hear, then bursting out in loud laughter.

ROSIE SIMPSON IN FRONT OF
NELLIE'S CELLAR DOOR

Because "Aunt Nellie" was very religious, the big girls couldn't do some things. She once walked all the way up to the schoolyard to see if her nieces were playing ball on Sunday. She didn't allow card playing, Dorothy said, so they played cards on a quilt in the side yard and hurriedly

JOAN SIMPSON ON NELLIE'S WALL

stuck the cards under the quilt when they saw her coming across the highway carrying her typewriter.

There were things her nieces couldn't get out of, such as the Sunday lunches with Maggie Abbett, where they had to sit like little ladies while the two women talked. And when Skyline Bill came to visit with Nellie—an unlikely combination—one of the girls had to sit in the house with them for appearance' sake, even on pretty days.

Nellie had a well in her backyard from which the girls pumped drinking water. Whenever a fishing worm appeared with the water, Nellie made the girls leave it in the bottom of the bucket. "It purifies the water," she told them.

Once in awhile I got to sit with the big girls in the evenings, on Nellie's wall at the corner steps where they watched cars go by. Sometimes, when the sun was about to set, they counted the number of drivers coming around the curve who reached up and pulled down their sun visors.

And yet people said there was nothing to do in a small town.

Harriet McKinney

Harriet McKinney's body was like a picture of a sky-scraper: the closer it got to the ground, the bigger it became, or maybe it just seemed that way because I was afraid of her. She, too, was a widow and lived in the next row house after Nellie's. Harriet's place was just one room wide, like ours, and there was only one front window to go with her front door. When Mr. Gannon came to visit her, she pulled down her window blind and we couldn't see anything. So we told everybody she didn't have a chaperon.

HARRIET McKINNEY, SMILING

Hers was one of the few old ladies' houses that was furnished to match the lady. Most of the other women were frail little things with furniture that couldn't have been budged by rampaging elephants. You always wondered why a ninety-pound woman needed such heavy furniture, but with Harriet, the heavy furniture seemed perfect.

She had a small patch of soil between her front window and the sidewalk and she grew ferns there because the sun never hit it. One day when I was coming home from the post office, *I walked through those ferns. I mashed some of them flat.* I don't know why I did it. I knew it was a bad thing to do even before I did it.

Unbelievable as it sounds, with her having just that one window and all those rooms lined up, she saw me and marched right down to our house. Daddy was in bed because he'd had his appendix taken out, so he couldn't spank me and I had to settle for a bawling out. He was pretty upset, though, and I thought it was awfully inconsiderate of Harriet McKinney to do that to a man who was in his sickbed.

But even while I was seeing these flaws, other people were seeing Harriet McKinney as interested in "furthering the cultural growth" of Vernon's children. Her front hall was full of library books rotated from the county library at North Vernon; Rosie Arney's boys came to her house with their guitars strapped to their backs; and she gave Bob Fry and other kids piano lessons.

Back when my aunts were in school they went to her house for meetings of the LTL. Aunt Naomi said the letters stood for Loyal Temperance Legion, a young ladies group sponsored by the Women's Christian Temperance Union. Their symbol was The Little Cold Water Girl.* They paid 10c per year dues, met monthly, and got free pins.

Mary Ale had belonged to the group. She said Harriet told the girls of the dangers of drink and trained them to make a great ceremony of stamping on cigarettes they saw on Vernon's sidewalks. Mary said, "That lady really tried to improve people and things."

Maybe that was my problem. I felt that Harriet McKinney saw in me a girl with no talent and that's why she

*PICTURED ON PAGE 264

51

didn't even *try* to teach me anything. I went to her house only to borrow library books.

Jacksons

We Spurlock kids weren't allowed to window peep, so when we walked past the Jackson house after dark, we walked v-e-r-y s-l-o-w-l-y. We wanted to see what it was atheists did. Much to our disappointment, we saw no fire-belching statues, no bubbling caldrons. The inside of their house always looked just like all the other houses in Vernon.

Prof Jackson, who said his religion was something called "altruism," would be in his living room chair, reading a newspaper or book under a brass floor lamp with a white pleated shade on it. In the dining room his divorced daughter Phyllis would be sitting at the table typing, or just staring at the typewriter through thick glasses under a green celluloid visor that reflected the ceiling light.

"This is how writers in Hollywood look," I'd whisper to Katie, then we'd take another step. "She's been to Hollywood, you know."

The Jacksons came to Vernon in 1910 and Phyllis graduated from Vernon High School four years later. Prof had already taught twenty-six years when he began at the Vernon Academy, serving as principal and teaching math, history, the sciences, and music. He coached sports and would say, when he caught any of the boys smoking, "If God had intended for you to smoke, he would have put smoke-stacks on your heads." A funny thing for an atheist to say.

V.H.S. lore was full of stories about Prof. According to one that I confirmed, he gave Dick Willman and some other high school boys a test tube during chemistry class and sent them to the restroom to fill it with warm water. The tube contained something besides warm water when they brought it back. Never one to let anybody get the drop on him, Prof held it up and said, "Just the right temperature."

Even when he wasn't on the scene he won the contest.

Lots of people told us about our daddy tipping over Prof's outhouse, then falling into the pit when he turned to run.

Prof was advisor of the high school newspaper when my mother was on the staff in the early 1930s. We liked to look at her old school papers. This is what Prof put in them about corrections:

> *It is a well known law of pedagogy that the best teaching is that which stimulates the most and best thinking on the part of the student. If a student knows that his copy will be corrected by a teacher before it is sent to the printer, he is likely to turn in a piece of work much inferior to what he is capable of doing. In order to stimulate our students to do their best work, we send their copy to the printer without making any corrections...In our school the work of the students is corrected in the English classes after it has been printed. Thus the writers are stimulated to put forth their best effort and all our students are benefitted by taking part in correcting their work.*
>
> *L. A. Jackson*

He was retired by the time we started school, but visited classes throughout our high school years and always left us pondering some great theory. It was Prof—that's what everybody called him—who told us a tree falling in a woods would not make a sound unless somebody was there to hear it. He told us nothing influences conduct except pleasure and pain. He asked, "How do you know if a color is really green?" and said, "When you become parents, never, ever make a threat to your child unless you are prepared to carry it through."

Because of his love for music, he was one of the most faithful attenders of the Vernon Presbyterian Church. He played any acceptable instrument in that church from spoons—or sticks he called "bones"—at a church party to a violin during worship hour. His favorite was the trombone. He directed the choir, too, but he always left when it came time for the sermon. Rev. Tull would wait patiently while Prof, at the back of the church, put on his coat, hat, galoshes, and gloves, then gathered up his instruments, music, and umbrella. After Prof had closed the door, Rev. Tull would start preaching.

The Presbyterian church was generous, allowing Prof to take part in Sunday school classes for awhile. After a time they asked him to quit because he was creating problems with his beliefs, starting a lot of arguments. He was hard to argue with. In their hearts the church people knew they were in the right, but, as one of them said, "Prof could talk better than we could."

He took extremely good care of his wife, who was in a wheelchair because she had been thrown by a horse. Sometimes we could see her sitting on the front porch. After she died, Prof would stroll around town and visit with former students. Aunt Vonda said he stopped by her house once, and said he had nothing to look forward to now that his wife was dead.

I don't think his daughter was an atheist; I believe she was a Christian Scientist. Phyllis did everything she could to bring culture to Vernon. She had no children of her own, but in the big parlor of the Jackson house she rolled back the rugs and taught singing and dancing to children from all over the county. She directed high school plays. The artist husband she had brought back from the West had helped her with these projects while he was doing some big paintings for the courthouse walls. They produced plays all over the county, but he soon grew bored with Vernon and left.

In the summer of my freshman year, Phyllis allowed any interested young person to be in a play. It didn't cost us a thing. I was inside the Jackson house a lot that summer.

We practiced about six weeks, then presented our play in the high school assembly room. She had done this same thing when my Aunt Betty was in high school. That group was called the Sindiana Players, a name probably thought up by Aunt Betty.

Phyllis taught me things about makeup. When I fretted about my lower lip being WAY BIGGER than my upper lip, and I knew everybody was looking at it and what could I do to make it look smaller, she told me to make my upper lip look larger. "Men like full-lipped women," she said. Hellen Ochs, one of the few Vernon mothers who wore makeup on weekdays, had told me to make my lower lip look smaller by using a lighter shade of lipstick on it, but Phyllis had been to Hollywood, so I followed her advice. No matter what I did, though, I still looked like a ten-year-old who had been into her mother's makeup.

I wore the same shoe size as Phyllis and she let me wear a pair of her shoes in the play—the first heels I had ever worn. She said I could borrow them anytime I wanted to. I never had occasion, but just thinking about those red heels waiting up there in her closet made me happy.

House of Clocks

Around noon was the best time to visit Lunsford's house. They were an old couple, but we didn't call them Mr. and Mrs. Lunsford. We called them Ma and Pap Lunsford because that's what Daddy called them. He had lived with them after his grandparents died. Her name was Maud but she didn't have an *e* on the end like Maude Rowan did. This was what a lot of farmers called their mules. The two ladies would send cards to each other that said "from one old mule to another."

Katie and I usually went to Lunsford's house by way of the alley. This was not only a shortcut, but avoided Frank Jordan's wallpaper store and him standing in the front door. Sometimes he would be sitting in front of his store, and Mr.

Huelson, the county school superintendent, would be sitting with him because his office was next door. Frank Jordan would sing, "Here comes Kitty and Catty." I didn't like this because I was the one he called catty. Even when we slipped through the alley, Frank Jordan could appear at the back door of his store or their upstairs apartment and yell, "There goes Kitty and Catty!" But he was far enough away I could pretend I didn't hear him.

WILFRED HUELSON AND FRANK JORDAN

If Pap was nearby when Ma Lunsford opened their front door, she always said the same thing: "Well, look who's here, Pap!" making our arrival seem like a happy event. When he wasn't in the front room, he probably was in his back room shop, repairing clocks or shoes. He seldom was on his feet because he had something wrong with his body. He walked slowly, leaning back, with his knees bent, and was known around kid circles as "the man who walked backwards." He didn't put his cane out in front like most men did; he put it behind himself to keep from tumbling over backwards.

Pap Lunsford was a man of few words. Usually he was sitting in an overstuffed chair in the corner playing solitaire on a bread board with his cane leaning nearby. He would respond to Ma's announcement like he thought our arrival was *not* a happy event. He usually buried his chin in his neck, looked out over his glasses, and grunted at us. Then he would glance toward the back hall like he was wondering if he'd locked his shop.

The first thing Katie and I did was hand Ma Lunsford the jigsaw puzzles we'd borrowed. Then we scanned the front room to see if any new faces had been added to the family photos. Yes, we did check out the shop, whether Pap was in there or not, but we never bothered anything. We just checked to see what was being built up or torn down and to see if that funny, upside down black foot was still sticking straight up in the air.

PAP LUNSFORD

On our way through the kitchen we looked to see if there was anything good in a carnival glass bowl sitting on the oilcloth covered table. If there was, and if we stared at it long enough, Ma would offer us some. We always said yes so as not to hurt her feelings. Usually, the contents of the bowl was some kind of stewed fruit. Old people stewed everything.

Clocks were not only in the shop, they were all over the house and we kept our eyes on them when the noon hour neared. Even though we were familiar with most of them, choosing the clock to stand by when the striking began wasn't an easy thing to do with butterflies in our stomachs.

Some clocks seemed to groan for five minutes before working up enough energy to strike, while others just rang out with no warning at all. When the orchestra finally did began to play, it hit every note on the scale, in sounds ranging from tiny, delicate dings to low, echoing gongs. Throw in a few cuckoos and a couple of cackling little girls running from room to room, and you have a scene of total madness.

When it was time for us to leave, we followed Ma into the bedroom where the puzzles were kept. We gasped every time she pulled back those flowered curtains and exposed shelves full of nothing but puzzles. Knowing our mother allowed only two or three at a time presented another difficult decision. Which would it be...the English cottage with the thatched roof? the fox hunt with all the bright, red coats? the ship of many sails on the whitecapped sea?

Sometimes Ma Lunsford gave us raw food out of her garden to take home to our mother, but vegetables in the garden weren't as fun as pie or cake in the kitchen. Then it was back through the alley to home and cleaning off the waterent table for a new puzzle. After many such trips I figured out how Frank Jordan knew we were running through that alley: he heard those puzzles rattling.

Laura Hess and Her Mama

Laura Hess was a spinster older than our parents. She lived on the top of the hill with her mother, Mrs. Carson, whom she called, "Mama." Mama was one of those old ladies who still wore long dresses. She walked with a crooked, gnarly cane. At mealtime Mama kept the bread on her lap. Anyone who wanted some had to ask her for it.

Mama could be in the house and hear her chickens make a certain noise that she knew meant *snake*. Even if she was eating supper, she'd hurry out into the backyard with a hoe or rake and kill it. Mama was kind of grouchy, but Laura, who had been a Vernon school teacher, was nice. She helped neighborhood school children with their homework.

Laura Hess and Mama owned all three things in our little song that began, "Come all ye playmates..." She had a rain barrel, a cellar door, and an apple tree. Katie and I rescued many a hop toad from that rain barrel, which sat at the corner of their big front porch overlooking the river and the cement bridge, one of the best front porches in Vernon. Laura Hess and Mama had a rose bush growing against a tree on the corner of their front yard and this bush was covered with tiny, yellow roses all summer. We didn't pick very many.

I suppose it was in this yard that the silverware was hidden during the Civil War when the South's General Morgan was coming. It wasn't there anymore, but there were plenty of other things to look at. In the yard formed by the "L" shape of the red brick house, a cistern pump stood on a square of concrete. Mornings, in early summer, this was a warm place to sit and examine the geodes and sea shells Laura had lined up around the edges of the slab.

LAURA HESS; DANNY STARK IN BACKGROUND

It's possible the Carson barn *was* left over from the 1860s. It was the biggest barn still standing in town, and still usable, not like Nellie Stout's barn that we were afraid would fall in on us. Laura no longer had a cow, but she had lots of chickens and sold eggs to people. Her backyard was full of tent-shaped brooding huts. She would let Katie and me gather eggs and look all over the chicken yard for hidden nests of "setting" hens. Those fat hens hid their nests well, sometimes sitting on twenty eggs at a time.

I visited this house often during the summer, when Laura's half-sister Margaret Adamaitis from Chicago came with her two daughters. One of them, Laura Belle, was my age and we spent much time together. At night, being allowed to play with a real flashlight, we sneaked all over that yard, mostly teasing our little sisters, Mary Lou and Mary Alice, until a *real* screech owl scared us inside.

Coming from a big city, Laura Belle could tell us things we didn't know. She told us the wool scarves we tied around our heads were called *babushkas*. Laura Belle had trouble sleeping in Vernon. She said Vernon was too quiet.

Robersons

Robersons lived just beyond Laura Hess in a brick house that had once been a school. Mary, Johnny, Edna, and Tommy were our age and we spent a lot of time with them, at their house and ours. Their oldest sister, Alice, worked in North Vernon and had a room there. She rode the bus home on Wednesdays, her day off. Alice sometimes had her camera with her and took a picture of us as she walked up the hill.

The best reason for going to Roberson's house in cold weather was to watch their dad butcher a hog, but I didn't go up there until I was sure it was already dead.

A PICTURE ALICE TOOK OF US ON THE SAWDUST PILE — *Front:* JOHNNY ROBERSON, TOMMY ROBERSON, AND RONNIE LAKE. *Back:* KATIE, MARY ROBERSON, AND ME

Dudley's lived in the house across the street halfway up the hill from us, the house where our mother once went to school. But they soon moved out and Charles "Froggy" Harris, a man new to Vernon, bought it. He moved in, along with his daughter, Hazel Lake, her sons Mark Rieser and Ronnie Lake, and her daughter Carol Lake, and Froggy's two dogs, Mush and Rum Boogie.

FROGGY HARRIS AND MUSH

Carol was beautiful, but shy and older than we were. We played cowboy and war with Ronnie and his cousin Bobby Miller, who sometimes came to visit in the summer. Bobby could yodel and he said bad words, like "Heck Fire."

Ronnie Lake had a problem. His body manufactured Tarzan yells all the time. They would build up inside him until he would have to let one out, no matter what the time or place. At least his mother usually knew where he was. Actually, he spent most of his time up at the poolroom Froggy ran on Front Street. When he was on his way home, even late at night, we could hear that Tarzan yell.

If coming home early on a winter evening, Ronnie would stop in on our front room, where we often had elaborate things built out of kindling sticks, including structures strong enough to stand on. (These were the narrow, curved pieces of wood cut out of the slats used in porch swing backs. Daddy brought them home from the factory, always reminding us, "They're full of splinters." In wintertime our mother used them for starting the fire every morning.) Ronnie Lake's surprise visits were the reason we

Spurlock girls locked the front door when we dressed behind the stove on cold mornings.

One afternoon when he stopped in, he got down on the floor to join in our play and his pants ripped. That incident went down in Spurlock history as "the day Ronnie Lake backed all the way home."

Bowerlys

Riley and Mable Bowerly lived right next to the cement bridge. Their two sons, Tom and Paul, were grown and married, but we didn't go to the Bowerly house to play with kids. We visited the two work horses in a small barn at the end of their lane, and the two pigs in a pen at the side of the barn.

It was hard to believe that lane was once the highway to Madison. A guard rail was built across the end of it now, where we could stand on a high, stone foundation left over from the iron bridge that was there when our mother was small.

The kids in our family had trouble pronouncing Riley Bowerly's name and called him everything from Roddy Body to Rollie Bollie. He never said very much, but we always knew when he was walking past our place because we could smell the Prince Albert tobacco he smoked in his pipe.

Riley Bowerly's wife, Mabel, was one of those sassy, skinny women who was hard to picture without a broom in her hand. We liked her though, because she let us use her yard. We could walk through her yard when we went down to play in the shallow water and sand bars under the first arch. And she would let us rake her leaves, then jump in them and rake them up again. Bowerly's yard sloped steeply, right down to the highway embankment that stopped our sleds after we slid all the way from the church and jumped the ditch. What a great yard.

Fishers

The Fisher kids, Jim, Ida Belle, and Bob, lived across the highway and we played with them sometimes. Their dad, who worked at the funeral home between our house and theirs, washed his car every single day. Fisher's brick house came all the way out to the sidewalk and they sat in front of it in those S-shaped, steel lawn chairs. Those chairs were ice cold, even on the hottest summer day. If I forgot and sat in one while wearing a bare midriff, I jumped right back out. At bedtime Fishers would turn them around and lean them against the house.

Because of Fisher's mother, Stella, I wanted to have hips. Stella had what was known as "a swing on her back porch," which I studied every day when she and Frank walked hand in hand to Nauer's Drugstore for ice cream cones. She was really good. She could make just the *hem* of her skirt swish back and forth.

VanGordens

Mr. and Mrs. VanGorden lived catty-cornered from Nauer's Drugstore and she had one of the nicest flower gardens in town. No matter how big of a hurry you were in, you just had to stop and look at it. It covered her entire backyard, all kinds of flowers enclosed in a scalloped wire fence. Mrs. VanGorden didn't want anybody picking her flowers. She didn't even pick them herself. When she wanted flowers for a vase, she asked her neighbor, Mrs. Welker, for some of hers.

I was never sure who all lived at VanGorden's. It was another one of those three-generation places. At least one daughter was back home, a widow with two sons named Bob and Butch Dawson, Butch being just a little older than I. His real name was Shirley, but nobody called him that except his mother and grandma.

When Butch was a little boy, he wore strings of safety pins around his neck when he came to Sunday School because he thought they looked nice. His fiddling with them nearly drove his teacher, Teenie Walt, crazy. She told him one day he might make her forget what she was going to say and Butch said, "That's all right with me."

Seeing him tethered to the clothesline pole in VanGordens' backyard hinted of trouble ahead. Sure enough, when he got older and was turned loose on Vernon, he played rough. Butch was racing around in the courtyard after dark one evening and couldn't see that somebody had left the handle sticking up on the drinking water pump. He ran his head right into that handle and cried all the way home, "Oh, I'm dying. Oh, I'm dying." His grandmother came out to meet him and took care of his wounds.

He must not have been hurt too badly, though; he went on to become a football hero at North Vernon High School.

MARY LOU IN NELLIE STOUT'S BACKYARD

PARTY LINE

The days of the one-digit number were long gone by the time we got our first telephone. Now calling someone was downright complicated. To reach us a person had to wait for the operator to say, "Number, please," then say to the operator, "158-R, one ring, please".

Being on a party line was one of the ways we got to know our neighbors, especially when a phone was left off the hook and we kids had to go from door to door asking, "Is your phone off the hook?" After we learned who was on our line, we usually could determine whose phone was off the hook by listening to voices and background noises.

The receiver left off the hook most often was at VanGorden's. This was good because we could tell by the loud ticktocking of Mrs. VanGorden's clock, or the sound of her on the back porch yelling, "Shirley! Get away from those flowers!" We knew when Mrs. VanGorden was listening in on our conversations and always wished we could see her face when we sang, "Hello, Mrs. VanGorden."

We Spurlock girls liked to have the phone cord running through our fingers while we talked, imagining we looked like Petty girls. Petty was the name of an artist whose pinup pictures often appeared in magazines. The gorgeous gals he drew were always holding telephones.

Our dad didn't use the phone very often, but when he did, he didn't like people listening in. So he would drop a clue to the person on the other end, then blow his crow

TRYING TO BE A PETTY GIRL

caller into the receiver as loudly as he could. There would be a sudden click and the ticktocking would stop.

We kids used to listen in *some*. We listened to Don "Pinky" Whiteaker talking to his girlfriend Marilyn. We could be anywhere in the house and listen to Grandma using our phone to talk to her sister in North Vernon. She always shouted because Aunt Murt was two miles away. She began every conversation with a loud "Is that you, Murt?" Her face would get red because she was not comfortable with the telephone, and she was constantly clearing her throat.

So whenever one of us got on the phone and had voice problems, somebody in the next room would yell, "Is that you, Murt?" Sisters are terrible.

KATIE (*right*) AND ME HOLDING A
TURTLE; OUR HOUSE IN BACKGROUND

THE MAXWELL

What did the Spurlocks have in common with Jack Benny? Well, we owned a Maxwell, that's what, a 1923 Maxwell convertible. The top was too rotten to raise up, so Daddy covered the car with a tarpaulin at night. That way the seats would be dry when he drove to work the next morning. If it wouldn't start, he'd find the steel, L-shaped thing called a "crank," stick it in the front of the car, turn it hard, and the car would start.

Every few years he got out his brush and enamel and painted the wheels fire engine red and the body apple green. It's a good thing there was a spare tire on the back of the car, because new tires were hard to find. Whenever the Maxwell needed a new tire, Daddy had Pat Fry, who worked in Chicago, bring one home on the weekend.

TEDDY ON THE MAXWELL

If there was a softball game going on at the school-yard, the Commons, or North Vernon's city park, the Maxwell went, loaded with us and our friends, because Daddy played on a team for years. He occasionally entertained the audience at the Commons by backing the Maxwell halfway up the railroad embankment, then coasting down. The Maxwell was indestructible.

FAYE TAYLOR

Sometimes I saw strangers laughing at our green and red car with the mommy and daddy and baby in the front and all the rest of the kids in the back. They didn't know that even our friends with nice cars loved to ride in it. But our friends didn't get to do one special thing.

Only Spurlock kids were in the back seat when we rode home at night from Cherry Park, a neighborhood several miles east of Vernon where our daddy grew up. We leaned back to see all the stars, and the top of Engle's bridge (while still laughing after hitting the big bump at the beginning), and eagerly looked forward to the ceiling of the culvert. Only Spurlock kids were there to groan when we got home.

AUNT VONDA AND THE MAXWELL IN THE LATE 1930s

VERNON SCHOOL

Grade School

All twelve grades being together was nice when we were little. If any of us had trouble adjusting to the first grade, the teacher went and got a big sister or brother to come and sit with us. Just seeing them during the noon hour helped us through the day.

A lot of country kids brought their lunches. We did, too, in bad weather. Our lunch sacks were all kept in the lockers at the back of the room, wooden closets with double doors on them, hooks inside, and shelves at the top. That end of the room always smelled like overripe bananas.

It wasn't an unpleasant smell. It was just a school smell, along with the traces of kerosene fumes on the kids who didn't have electricity, the oranges we got at Christmas, the thousand layers of varnish on our wooden desk tops, the smell of boys' gym shoes that never got washed, and the oil on the dust mops.

We choked on this oil smell when we had to go into the dark broom closet every year, one at a time, and sit under a blue light. But worse than the smell was the pain, when Mrs. Binford, the county nurse, scraped around on our heads with toothpicks, looking for ringworms, nits, and cooties.

Every day at lunchtime some of the little kids had pennies in their pockets and asked the big kids who went downtown to shop for them. The big kids were handy in a lot of ways, but sometimes they almost ran over us when we were coming in from recess the same time they were changing classes.

Mrs. Reese was probably my most special grade school teacher, and because of some rearranging, my class got to have her twice, in the second and fourth grades. She was a small woman who kept a Bible on her desk, but was capable of being feisty and once jerked a boy right out of his shoes.

When we brought in our Christmas presents the year I was in fourth grade, I couldn't find one under the tree for me. Even when they were all handed out, I still didn't have one and felt tears starting to burn in my eyes. Then, while the other kids were all playing with their toys, Mrs. Reese slipped me out into the hall, where she reached down into a dark corner and picked up a present. "I drew your name," she said. "I'll give this to you when it's time to go home."

After the other kids had left—thank goodness we got out at noon—Mrs. Reese gave me the present and I ran home and opened it. It was a cardboard doll house and furniture, all for me to put together. The house even had a stairway in it. I could see that it cost a *lot* more than we were supposed to spend on our names and I took very good care of it.

VERNON SCHOOL

In the winter, when the snow was just right on Madge Jordan's hill, we brought our sleds to school and used them during recess and lunch hour. Some of the teachers slid with us. Donnie Layman and other hot-shot boys, who constantly worked on their runners with sandpaper and steel wool instead of the usual bee's wax, could start at the Presbyterian Church and slide all the way to the end of Dryden's bridge. If the river was frozen, they slid down through Old Johnny Jones's garden and out onto the ice.

William Stewart allowed the kids who rode his bus to bring their sleds to school. They had it made on the trip home, when he stopped at the top of the long hill by Randall's house and let the kids with sleds get off, then picked them up at the bottom.

Towards the end of World War II an exciting thing happened during recess that had nothing to do with sledding. We were playing in the locust grove behind the gym when Juanita Fitch and a few other kids saw some men who had the letters P.O.W. on the backs of their shirts. There were two or three of them and they ran over the deep bluff behind the school. The teacher called the sheriff. When he came to the school she said, "I know this is true because it was told to me by my most honest and reliable student." But the men were never found.

Junior High

By the time we got to junior high school, the little kids were kind of a nuisance...always underfoot when we went to classes in the square building, or tying up the stalls in the rest room. And there was nothing like hurrying to a water fountain between classes only to find a long line of short people getting drinks. Worst of all, we could hardly get past the end of the sidewalk at noon because they would be waiting with their pennies for us to buy them Guess Whats and B-B-Bats and Tootsie Rolls. They'd jump in front of us yelling, "Are you going downtown?" "Are you going downtown?"

But, yet, the place would have been empty without them. Winter wouldn't have been winter without the Bon

Ami snowflakes on Mrs. Reese's windows. As high school students we looked up at those snowflakes and laughed at the times we dabbed those same panes ourselves. Sometimes we forgot to act as if we were no longer grade school kids, like when there was a litter of new kittens in the furnace room.

I loved to hear the little ones singing in the spring, when their windows were decorated with tulips and pushed open. I looked forward to skipping classes to help their teachers with costumes for the spring festival. Sitting outside on the steel fire escapes that looked like they were held onto the building with two bolts, we older girls hand-sewed crepe paper skirts and hats that looked like flowers. The spring festival, held in the gym, was one of the most beautiful events in Vernon...Maypole dances, swings with flower covered ropes that went all the way up to the rafters, every child dressed in a costume.

Junior high study hall took place in the assembly, a room on the top floor that went all the way across the back of the older building. The worst thing about this room were the pictures of earlier graduating classes that lined the walls. If we looked up from our work, our parents were looking back down at us, every hour, every day.

When I was in junior high, the principal and teachers decided Vernon School should have a band. Grades four through nine were gathered into the assembly room where a man using a piano, a violin, and a coronet gave something called "The Pan-American Music Aptitude Test." Not long after that a stranger came to our house. We kids were sent outside, so I didn't know what his visit was about. When I read in the high school newspaper that I had been the only student to get a perfect score on the test, I figured out that the stranger was a seller of musical instruments. I knew my parents couldn't afford an instrument, so I understood why nobody ever asked me if I wanted to be in the band.

Well, I knew they could afford a twirling baton, and that I could teach myself to use it. When Santa Claus brought me one for Christmas, I didn't even see anything else I got, just that shaft of shiny chrome with the white rubber tips on the ends. I used some baby-sitting money for material and made me a uniform out of white satin with all the trimmings. By the time the band was ready to march, I was ready to lead them. Except for that Indianapolis parade, where my group watched helplessly while I marched backwards a third of the way into the band in front of us, I had a great time.

At the end of our seventh grade, Mrs. Dawson retired. She had graduated from Vernon High School in 1900 and moved back to Vernon to teach in 1931. She taught English, Latin, and music. Even when kids gave her a hard time, she was always cheerful. She thought the world and everything in it was beautiful.

One of the reasons kids gave her a hard time was because of the songs she made us sing, things like "Bring the Torch, Jeannette Isabella," "Santa Lucia," and the fox hunt song that began, "Do ye ken John Peale at the break of day?" She had a little thing she called a pitch pipe that she blew one note on before every song.

Our new music teacher was just out of college and let us sing modern songs along with the old ones. She directed a spring variety show on the assembly stage her first year at Vernon. Before it started I peeked out the curtains and saw Mrs. Dawson sitting on the front row. I was concerned about what she would think of us eighth grade girls singing "If," "The Thing," "My Heart Cries for You," "To Think

You've Chosen Me," and "Nevertheless." When we ended our part by acting out "The Aba Daba Honeymoon," Dorothy was sitting down in the audience laughing so hard tears were running down her cheeks. The best part, though, was seeing Mrs. Dawson swinging her foot and tapping her toes, all through the program.

High School

As if becoming freshmen wasn't exciting enough, we got to look over the new crop of kids coming in from Bigger and Sandcreek Townships. As soon as those buses landed on the first day of school, we lined the front hall of the gym. The boys looked the new girls over and we girls looked the new girls over. (Well, what fourteen-year-old girl who grew up in the county seat, even the smallest county seat in the state, is going to be interested in a boy who still scoots his desk around while making motor noises with his mouth?!)

So while the boys were looking over the new girls and saying, "*There's* a cute one," we girls were saying, "There's a *cute* one." They were a threat, that's what they were. But during the next four years friendships were forged that would last lifetimes.

And a funny thing happened to those new boys on their way through high school. It was amazing how interesting they became. One of them ended up being good looking, president of the senior class, a basketball player, and in search of a date for the prom.

We freshman girls said, at least out loud, that we weren't even in the running, so we were shocked when he asked our friend and classmate, Cynthia Crist. We thought it was awful of him to ask a freshman girl when so many junior and senior girls didn't have dates, but we weren't jealous or anything.

I took Home-Ec all through high school, even though I was convinced the teacher didn't like me. My problems with her started when we were freshman and getting ready to buy blouse patterns. She was measuring what she called our "busts" and was shouting our measurements to a girl she'd asked to write them down *on the other side of the room.*

As I feared, I was one of only two girls whose measurements were still in the twenties. "Twenty-eight!" the teacher yelled when she did me. The grade school kids playing in the shelter house probably heard her. (If she hadn't pulled that tape so tight I would have been an easy thirty.)

Shirley Cornett was the other girl still in the twenties and she ended up with the best figure in the class. I was thankfully but barely able to pitch my undershirt and order a strapless bra from Sears by the time I went to my first prom.

I knew I wasn't helping my relationship with the home-ec teacher by marching to my own drum, but, darn it, I had been making blouses and gathered skirts for years, and my mother thought we should be learning more practical things. She gave me an old wool suit to rip up and I made a lined coat and matching hat for my little brother Joe to wear to church.

In Home-Ec we girls learned the importance of wearing girdles when we dressed up and went out in public, to keep under control the vast movements of our thirty inch hips. We learned that nice girls didn't wear skirts that were tight enough to "cup" under the backside.

Are You Now or Have You Ever Been...

In the 1950s, somebody decided the high school history and government classes should witness history being made. They borrowed a TV set from a North Vernon dealer and installed it on the gym stage and pulled the front and back curtains. Every day we watched something called "the McCarthy Hearings." Or rather, we were supposed to be watching them.

It was distracting to be sitting on that dark stage with boys, so we girls looked at them instead of Senator Joe McCarthy. We stared at their profiles and the backs of their necks. We dressed them with our eyes, imagining them in suits that were all one color; crisp, starched white shirts with gold cuff links; neckties that tied instead of clipped on and were held down with gold bars that matched the cuff links; black polished shoes...

We couldn't have cared if anybody in the whole world was or ever had been a member of the Communist Party. This extremely boring project was probably arranged by The Principal. Senator McCarthy was his hero. He once said to our government class, "Franklin Delano Roosevelt is burning in Hell!" Joyce Whitcomb told her dad at supper that evening and, being a Democrat, he wasn't too pleased.

Sometimes when I got bored during senior government class, I'd put my left elbow on my desk and my engagement ring up to my eye. I'd be slowly wiggling the ring with my thumb to make the colors in the diamond change when The Principal, out of the blue, had us put our heads down on our desks while he said a prayer for our country. Praying wasn't foreign to us—every kid in the class went to church someplace—but we always felt funny doing it in government class.

Prom Time
or
Did Anybody Ever Actually Go to Louisville?

It's a wonder we got to have proms at all; we didn't get to have any other dances. That s why, about three weeks before the happy event, Mrs. Hyder, who taught English-literature, sacrificed her lunch hour in trying to teach us the basic steps of ballroom dancing. I felt sorry for the boys when I looked down at their clodhoppers and tennis shoes trying to form that box waltz...one...two...three... "No, like this: one...two...three..." I felt sorry for Mrs. Hyder, too.

76

In 1954, when my class gave the prom, all the girls volunteered to be on the decorating committee because the decorators were allowed to break the no-pants rule and wear jeans to school. (But we had to restrict ourselves to the gym so we wouldn't contaminate the other girls.)

Decorating was one of the few ways we could use our artistic talents because there were no art classes in Vernon school once you got out of elementary. (I didn't want anybody to know I could draw anyway. I remembered how Dorothy used to talk about boys trying to get her to draw pictures of naked women.)

That same year the faculty decided we should use part of our hard-earned money to throw a dinner before the prom. Those of us who rebelled were sent straight to the principal's office. When a brave senior girl announced she would skip the dinner and come to the prom, a new rule was made: No come to dinner, no come to dance. Another rule was made, too, because Der Inspector didn't like dancing. "If I see one thing out of line on that dance floor, I'm going to come right out and tap you on the shoulder and out you'll go."

We really rebelled then. Bob Fry whispered, "We dare defend our rights!" The boys wore their shirt collars straight up in the back while we girls didn't speak to The Principal for a week. One brazen thing we did was wear our penny loafers with no socks. We *wanted* to commit that most punishable offence in Vernon High School, which was to walk on the gym floor in our street shoes, but I was afraid there would be a piano bench kind of lineup on the stage.

Our rebellion was fruitless. Prom night began with the dinner. We were all herded into the cafeteria, a separate building, an old army barracks, in fact, made of particleboard. The outside of this particleboard held the sun's heat until midnight while the inside absorbed grease like an ink blotter. Anyone who ever ate there in a mixed crowd knew the tables were a popular lovers' lane for fruit flies.

The tables were picnic style with continuous, step-over benches. In seating ourselves, we girls felt like old sows trying to change positions without mashing any piglets. The nylon net layers of our skirts that weren't held down by splinters puffed up to our chins and strained our gravy. After the dinner the teachers were full and happy, our dates were full and happy, but we girls were steamed. We grumbled all the way back to the gym while picking noodles out of our corsages.

But then the band started playing our theme, "Stairway to the Stars." We forgot our shiny faces and became quite beautiful, some of us in long dresses, some in ballerina length; the short girls in spike heels; the tall ones in ballerina shoes. (In spite of all the ballerina talk, I never saw anything on the gym floor that resembled ballet, unless it was the year that awful North Vernon boy spiked our punch.)

About halfway through the evening the big question would start cropping up, "Whatcha doin' after the prom?" There was always a lot of talk about "runnin' down to Louisville."

The three proms I attended were with Don Layman, and after every one of them we started toward Louisville but turned around along about Commiskey. All the way back to Vernon I made him promise not to tell anyone I had to be home on prom night—that's *in* the house—by one o'clock in the morning.

1954 PROM — JUANITA FITCH, DON LAYMAN, ME, AND DEAN SPEER

The following Monday the cool dudes were the guys who walked around the halls combing their hair and saying, "Went to Louisville after the prom." I always wondered, though, did anybody ever actually go to Louisville?

OTHER SPECIAL PLACES

The Vernon Baptist Church

When you're a child, you go to church for different reasons than you will as an adult. Besides going to learn about Jesus, you go to church so you can dress up. You go so you can sing hymns like "The Church in the Wildwood." You go to do fun things in Sunday School class and bring your papers home to make into a book. You go to hunt eggs the Saturday before Easter and get an orange and a sack of candy on Christmas Eve. You go because your parents make you go. Then you get older and attend B. Y. F. in the evenings because cute boys will be there, and the sponsors have parties.

When I was a teenager I occasionally went up to the churchyard alone on weekday nights to get out of our noisy house and think and pray, just as a Vernon girl might have done a hundred years before. I don't know how the church-yard looked then, but in the 1950s, the grass under those maple trees was softer than other grass, and the corner streetlight shining through the leaves made a lacy design on it. I felt closer to God when I walked around in the church-yard.

MRS. WELKER, MRS. LUNSFORD, AND MRS. CARTWRIGHT AT A CHURCH PICNIC

Sometimes church women prepared pitch-in dinners that we ate in the churchyard. It was a beautiful sight, breezes fluttering the edges of white cloths held down on long tables by dishes and dishes of food. The only thing that could ruin it was rain, or Jake Swarthout stirring his food together because "it's all going to the same place anyway." Kids didn't sit next to him because he would do the same thing to their food.

Only men and big boys were strong enough to ring the church bell, which they did by pulling on a rope inside the front door. If we got up the hill in time, we could hold on to the rope and get lifted way up off the floor. It was fun but scary. Sometimes church boys sneaked up to the top of the belfry. They said our bell had a hammer thing on it for tolling funerals. Every time the church bell rang, the beagle hounds chained up in our backyard howled and cried until it stopped. Daddy said it hurt their ears.

All the people in the church had regular places to sit. Sometimes a visitor would come in for church before Sunday School was out and accidentally get somebody's regular place. It looked funny to see that person have to sit somewhere else.

Gertrude Holmes sat in the aisle in her wheelchair. She had some kind of a disease that took away her muscle control. She tried to talk, but her tongue seemed too big and we couldn't understand her. Her mother was dead and her father a retired preacher. He pushed that wheelchair up the hill every Sunday. Their house caught fire one winter night and Gertrude was sitting in her wheelchair in the yard crying.

GERTRUDE HOLMES

When Rev. Holmes was no longer able to take care of her, he took her to the Muscatatuck State School near Butlerville. There was nothing wrong with Gertrude's mind, but this was the only place he could take her. When church women went out there to visit Gertrude, she seemed happy.

There were plenty of things in church to stare at. Our pews were very old. The seat of each one was made of a single wide board and the back was made of another wide board. A spindle rail ran all along the top. They were narrow and designed for sitting up straight.

The sanctuary ceiling was made of embossed tin that curved down at the edges instead of forming right angles. All our windows were green stained glass. In the summer Norman Cartwright, known as "Mose," used a long pole with a hook on the end to open the square windows above the main windows. We couldn't help

REV. HOLMES

with this job, or with winding the pendulum clock on the wall.

I liked to stare at church women. On hot Sundays they cooled themselves with fans furnished by Bolser and Shaw Monuments, or Jordan's Funeral Home. The fans were made of flat pieces of cardboard stapled to large Popsicle-type sticks and had religious pictures on them. The women also nursed their babies in church, but they covered the babies' heads with handkerchiefs. I liked to stare at Mrs. Welker's daughter Frances. She was a beautiful brunette who had an important job at the Indianapolis Motor Speedway and visited her parents on weekends. The Welkers came from one of the families that started our church in 1816.

When my friend Cynthia Crist and I were eleven years old, we were attending church as well as Sunday school. We went because we wanted to, but often found our minds wandering during the sermons. About halfway through we started listening for those three special words: "Let us pray."

I was spending a lot of time at her house and her mother started talking to us about taking our religion seriously and being baptized. Cynthia did it first, but I, while wanting to, held back until one evening during a revival in the spring after my twelfth birthday. Mrs. Crist was sitting behind me and during the hymn of invitation she reached up and pecked me on the back and I went forward.

On July 24, 1949, I walked down to Engle's bridge, where Mary Lou Patterson and I, girls in white dresses, were baptized in the Muscatatuck River. We changed clothes in the Clendenning house. When I got home, carrying my rolled-up towel under my arm, Mom was nursing Joe Eddie,

who was a brand new baby. I hung my wet clothes and towel on the line in the backyard, a little disappointed that I didn't really feel any different. I had not realized yet that baptism was a beginning and not an end.

Front Street

The row of brick buildings facing the courthouse was called Front Street, even though the street was really named Pike. This entire street was occupied by businesses, with two important buildings serving as bookends—Nauer's Drugstore and the post office. Because Front Street faced eastward and was sunny, we sometimes used that route to go to the post office on cool mornings instead of cutting through the courtyard.

MRS. CLENDENNING

That's what I was doing the morning I saw a new cardboard sign in the drugstore window that ruined my whole day. It was Dorothy Collins, the main girl singer on *Your Hit Parade*. She was wearing a sheer, light blue blouse and had her blond hair in her usual pageboy style. But she was holding a lit cigarette between her fingers, a Lucky Strike, and it just made me sick. I never thought as much of Dorothy Collins again.

L. to R.: FRONT STREET, CULVERT, VANGORDEN'S, AND A
VERNON BOY WALKING DOWN HILL

We didn't use Front Street on hot mornings because
the sidewalk burned our bare feet. It was bad enough having
to play hopscotch around the tobacco spit and walk around
the semi-circle of dead flies in front of the poolroom, where
Charles "Muggy" Hartwell would be sitting on the bench
clutching a swatter. Screen wire ends stuck out of the
swatter, and the bias tape binding was all frayed, but he was
good with it.

After the drugstore corner came Jim Boggs's garage,
with gas pumps in front of a big door, the biggest hole on
Front Street. Men loafed around here. I never understood
why men said their wives were lucky because they got to stay
home all day. When men *could* be staying home, they went
to some garage or filling station and loafed.

Next was Kirkham's electric and gift store, a strange
combination, then Calvert and Hunt's Groceries, Meats, and
Dry Goods. People who listened to Amos 'n' Andy on the
radio called it the "John Downs Store." Girls whose grand-
pas didn't own stores worked here. One of them said Paul

Hunt asked her why she always stopped and washed her hands after pumping kerosene. "Because my mother says our lunch meat tastes like kerosene," she answered.

We bought a few things at Hunt's. Katie was sent up there to buy some cheese once and was so nervous about being in a bigger store she couldn't remember the word *cheese* and asked for yellow meat. Women weighed their babies at Hunt's, just like they did at our store and Shaw's.

Calvert and Hunt's generated a lot of excitement one summer by placing a Wolverine work shoe, frozen in a block of ice, on the sidewalk in front of their store. The person who correctly guessed when that ice would melt and reveal a perfectly unharmed shoe would win a prize. I didn't win.

Across the alley was Billy Wenzel's Hardware, a pair of long, dark rooms full of shelves and pigeonholes. It was

always cool in the summer, and smelled of the linseed oil on the floorboards. Girls liked to look at the tiny Pyrex baking dishes and boys liked the cane poles and tackle. All of us liked to look at Mr. Wenzel in his hardware store apron. The best thing in there, though, was the Red Ryder Daisy air rifle.

Paul Hunt—we kids called him by his first name because he drove a school

PUMP CALVERT, NAOMI JOHNSON, PAUL HUNT, AND SHOE IN ICE

bus—and Mr. Wenzel both owned identical blue Buicks that could be seen parked near their stores. One day Paul Hunt

Right: INSIDE OF HUNT'S STORE 1/28/40 - *L. to R.*: PUMP CALVERT, PAUL HUNT, JOE DORGAY, A BAKER BOY, AND SAM LIESURE

came out of his store and got into Billy Wenzel's car, put his key in the ignition, and drove it home, where he was surprised to find his own blue Buick parked in the driveway.

Salty Hartwell owned the poolroom before Froggy did. Salty had a barbershop in the front room, the poolroom was in the middle room, and men played poker in the back room. Sometimes Vernon people would call the sheriff and say, "Men are playing poker at the poolroom," and the sheriff would answer, "I play poker there myself."

When Salty was playing poker and in came a barbershop customer, he'd say, "Deal me in; I'll be back in a minute." He once gave Bobby Linney such a bad haircut Bobby's mother came in and sassed him good. I always wished I could go in there and see Happy Hartwell asleep on the pool table.

After Jordan's wallpaper store closed, Everett Bare opened a wallpaper store next to the poolroom. He usually was sitting in front of it in a lawn chair and owned some real nice binoculars he'd let us look through anytime we wanted to. He liked giving Teddy a nickel just to hear Teddy say he was going to "take it down to Shotgun's and bend it."

The grownups said something about Everett Bare we didn't understand. They said his wife didn't

WENZEL'S HARDWARE AFTER IT WAS BOUGHT
BY O.E. BARNES, *pictured*

care if he slipped around Vernon's alleys all night, so long as he didn't get her rugs dirty when he came home.

THE POOLROOM — HOMER ROGERS, JESSE CLARKSON, MUSH, AND MARK RIESER

Front Street was an important part of a night game played by Vernon boys, and a few girls. Their "board" sometimes included all the town and the cemetery. They called their game "slips," because two teams tried to elude each other, give each other the slip. If somebody hit you on the back and said, "One, two, three, slips," you were out. On Front Street, where they scampered across the tops of buildings, they kept a board on Hunt's or Wenzel's store for crossing the alley in the middle of the block. Whichever group got across first pulled the board over with them.

Nauer's Drugstore

Mr. Nauer—if you wonder how to pronounce his name, it rhymes with *sour*—had run Vernon's drugstore since the beginning of time and his ads always contained the same four words: WE WANT YOUR TRADE. When children came into his store for the first time, he demanded to know their names, where they were from, and the names of their parents. Then he would wait on them.

Mr. Nauer was the only merchant on Front Street who wore a bow tie. He wore a lot of tweed in the winter, and elastic rings called sleeve garters on his arms, I guess to keep

87

his cuffs out of the ice cream containers. When my generation first encountered him, his wife was dead and he was already in his eighties, but he worked very briskly.

Older people seemed to take him alright, although he once bawled out nice Lucille Bolser because she came in at closing time. When we complained about him they said he just didn't like standing and waiting for kids clutching warm pennies to make decisions in front of the candy case. While this was going on, they said, he was missing a baseball game coming over the radio in his back room, or, if it was winter, he was too far from his potbellied stove.

His chair was beside the stove and in line with the main part of the store so he could see who came in the front door. It was a deep-seated, upholstered chair with an old blanket over it. A person of normal weight would have sunk all the way to the floor in that chair, but nobody except Mr. Nauer ever sat in it.

We could only steal glances of his mysterious office room back there, on the highway side of the building...shelves and shelves of old medicine bottles with gold labels on them. The ones in the windows could be seen from the sidewalk, too. Although Mr. Nauer no longer mixed up prescriptions, he still hung onto the old scales and mortar apparatus and measuring cups. An old Wells-Fargo safe taller than we were stood beside his rolltop desk.

There was a solid oak telephone booth out in the main part, behind the wrapping counter. It had narrow little windows in it. Between that and the soda fountain were two or three ice cream table sets, the kind with chairs that had backs made of heavy steel wires shaped like hearts. But if we bought anything from the fountain, we took it to the booths on the "other side," reached by passing through a huge archway.

This side was dark because of big cardboard signs in the windows and just a few bare light bulbs hanging down from a high ceiling. And somewhere up there were a couple of old slow-moving ceiling fans covered with oily dust. The long glass cases on this side of the store contained valuable things like jewelry and perfume.

The booths were made of dark, unpadded wood, almost black from years of varnish. They were high-backed. You couldn't see who was in the next one unless you looked before you sat down, and it was almost impossible to hear other conversations. There were about two inches of gum stuck under the booth tables, but you did not carve your initials in Mr. Nauer's furniture.

Six times a day the drugstore got busier because that's how many times the White Star bus stopped on its runs between Madison and Indianapolis. If the bare, yellow light bulb outside the first window was not on, the bus didn't stop, unless somebody was getting off. Alice Roberson's coming home on Wednesdays gave us a reason to meet the bus.

MR. NAUER
CARRYING HIS LUNCH TO WORK

In the late 1940s J. W. Coombs' mother, Ruth, worked in the drugstore and they lived on the second floor, so J. W. got the job of starting a coal fire every winter morning in the potbellied stove. Then he swept the floor and filled the pop machines. That stove was the only source of heat in the entire drugstore.

The third floor of the drugstore was called the *Odd Fellows Hall*. You could sneak up there and play with odd things. Some kids would put on fringed costumes and sashes and have sword fights with real swords while other kids made silent movie music on the grand piano.

On Wednesday afternoons one of Mr. Nauer's friends, Roy Hinchman, president of North Vernon's First National Bank, would come into the drugstore. He was the only person besides Mr. Wenzel, Bob Matthews, and Mr. Nauer's brother who called Mr. Nauer "Bill." It always sounded funny for somebody to call Mr. Nauer "Bill." In Mr. Nauer's little room, Mr. Hinchman would sit in the other chair, a leather one with wide, wood armrests, and these two men would visit and gossip. Mr. Nauer knew every closet in Vernon that had a skeleton in it. Well, some people knew that Mr. Nauer used snuff!

Graduating from penny candy, we grew tall enough to appreciate the coolness of the soda fountain's marble top, where we laid our sweaty forearms while watching Mr. Nauer make us nickel ice cream cones. He never stacked the ice cream like his help did when he wasn't there. We got the most ice cream when Virginia Tull waited on us because she was our big sister's friend. When Mr. Nauer was there, he watched his help closely while they filled the ice cream scoop. "Straight across," he would remind them, "and only one scoop in a milk shake or soda." According to a rumor that couldn't be confirmed, he melted down stale Hershey bars and sold them as chocolate blocks.

He sold regular Cokes, chocolate Cokes, cherry Cokes, vanilla Cokes, and something he called a marshmallow Coke that had all four in it. We kids called it a "suicide Coke." He once refused to sell one to Susie Rogers. "No," he said when she ordered it, "makes too much of a mess." Maybe that's where the suicide part came in...not in the drinking, but in the asking. On another hot summer day when Mary Hulse was buying her son a third ice cream cone, Mr. Nauer bawled her out. He said, "You shouldn't buy that baby so many ice cream cones!"

When we entered puberty, Mr. Nauer hampered our education by refusing to oil the hinges on the front door of the drugstore. This door, made of heavy glass with a thick wood frame around it, opened back against the magazine rack on the corner wall. Browsing in the drugstore we could see clearly the tempting magazine fronts, but didn't dare move that creaky door just to scan through them or he would look right over there.

The problem was that my girlfriends and I didn't know what men looked like naked. No photographs were available anyplace for us to look at, not even behind that door. There was, however, one small magazine called *Sexology Today* that answered readers' questions and, better yet, contained line drawings.

Thank goodness even Mr. Nauer had to eat sometimes, and when he went home for supper between five-thirty and six-thirty, we pounced on those little magazines and took them back to the booths in the other room. We had to take turns so somebody could stand watch. We also made it a point to find out when he went to North Vernon to do his banking. By the time we got through with those magazines they were so dog-eared and chocolate-smeared he probably never sold a one.

The girls who worked in the drugstore said Mr. Nauer never smiled, but whenever his only child, Martha, came to town, he beamed from ear to ear. Martha was a rich, single, husky-voiced woman who wore fur coats and lots of makeup. She was smart and had an important job as some kind of an auditor for the government.

The help liked it when Martha came home for visits because every day she was in Vernon, Mr. Nauer would go home for supper and not come back until closing time. Anybody who got near him then could tell he'd been drinking a bit. On one of Martha's visits, Virginia Tull, a preacher's daughter, borrowed *God's Little Acre* from the pocketbook display behind the creaky door and read it from cover to cover and all the covers in between.

I guess Mr. Nauer had his good points. He once ran a man out of his drugstore for saying something about Vernon that wasn't very nice. And if you were a dog, and your master was Frank Jordan, you could come in there with your master and get an ice cream cone. When my aunt Vonda worked for him in high school, he let her choose *anything* in the whole store for a Christmas present.

Another nice thing about Mr. Nauer was that he had a swinging, metal Coca-Cola sign outside at the corner of the building. Tall boys could jump up and slap that sign and make a big noise. By the time Mr. Nauer got to the door, it had stopped swinging. Everybody, if anybody was around, looked innocent...or did everybody look guilty? Either way, he couldn't tell who had done it.

The best thing about Mr. Nauer, though, was that he *did* have Prince Albert in a can.

The Post Office

Vernon people divided themselves into three different churches, three different grocery stores, and about that many places to eat lunch. But the one place where *every* family sent a representative was the post office. For our family, the post office would've been a two-block walk if we hadn't taken the shady path through the courtyard, a path that was probably caused by people walking to the post office. According to Vernon legend, our mother and daddy fell in love while walking together to the post office every evening.

I got to walk to the post office *one* time with my hair unbraided. I accomplished this by pestering my mother and getting out her album and showing her a picture of herself at my age with her hair unbraided. "I can tell because it's wavy all the way down to your waist," I said.

So on this morning I took the long way to get the mail, looking at myself in every store window on Front

Street. I stopped completely when I reached the window on Hunt's dry goods and notions side. Two strips of material in the latest and brightest colors I had ever seen—fuchsia and chartreuse—came down to a "V" inside the window and framed the reflection of my movie star face. I pulled my hair over one eye and did, in fact, look just like Veronica Lake. Suddenly my eyes refocused and I saw that some woman in the store was staring back at me and I ran all the way to the post office.

When we first started getting the mail, our mother had to help us across the highway. By the time we were old enough to go by ourselves, we were getting mail for other people, too, like our grandpa and uncle. Knowing several mailbox combinations was a pretty important job.

In the winter we picked up Nellie Stout's mail. She was very honest, insisting on paying us right then. We shivered on her front step while she searched every coin purse and sugar bowl in that big house. When she came back to the door with a couple of pennies she always said the same thing: "I might die tonight and I don't want to leave this world owing any money." We thought it was strange that leaving the world not owing two pennies was more important than mak- ing little girls freeze to death.

Doro- thy saved the pennies she earned this way for dime stamps to buy herself

L. to R.: POST OFFICE, DRIVERS ED CAR, RAT ROW, AND SHAW APARTMENTS

a war bond. When she was getting ready to go to Oklahoma and visit Aunt Betty, she cashed in her war bond and had money to buy a permanent.

Some adults got other people's mail. Charles "Muggy" Hartwell got the mail for several ladies in his end of town. One afternoon a substitute from North Vernon was running the post office when Charles came in and laid his paper sack in the window. The man raised his hands up over his head!

Mrs. Trapp ran the post office when we were little. Our mother hated to have to buy money orders, because Mrs. Trapp's fingers were all swollen with arthritis and it was such a struggle for her to fill them out. For a long time we thought Mrs. Trapp was George Washington. She had the same white hairdo and looked like he did in his picture high on the wall. Since we never saw her outside the post office, we knew only the part of her body framed in that postmaster's window, the same section we saw of George Washingon's body. We looked up at George Washington, then we looked at Annie Trapp, back and forth, back and forth. Yes, they were one and the same.

Not very many Vernonites congregated in the post office while the morning mail was being put in the boxes. But for the evening mail, the whole town seemed to gather in that not-very-big lobby (and not everybody used Lifebuoy to fight B. O.).

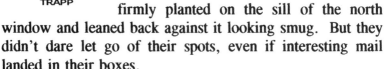

ANNA
"GEORGE
WASHINGTON"
TRAPP

People lined the walls, trying not to block the outside door. A few stood around the writing stand, careful not to get a lot of unwanted attention by kicking the green metal wastebasket. Of course, the first arrivals already had their elbows firmly planted on the sill of the north window and leaned back against it looking smug. But they didn't dare let go of their spots, even if interesting mail landed in their boxes.

The front windows went almost to the floor, with black wrought iron bars on the outside to keep anybody from breaking in and stealing our mail. The building had been a bank before it was a post office, and before that it was a circle store, called that because the shelves were built in a circle.

While the mail was being put into 200 boxes, conversations hummed, interrupted only by news of greater importance, which swept through the lobby like leaves blowing across the courtyard.

"Granny Jones died?"

"Well, at least she enjoyed ninety years of poor health."

"He what?"

"Cut off some fingers."

"Well, you don't just pick up a lawn mower while it's still running."

". . . and she has blue eyes, like her mother's, and..."

Vernon didn't need a newspaper.

Sometimes, though, everybody just stood and stared and the lobby was so quiet you could hear a stomach growl. We stared at the glass windows in the doors of our boxes, waiting for that special letter to slip in there, or a pink card that read PARCEL TOO LARGE FOR BOX, meaning a Sears order had finally arrived, or a package from Aunt Betty.

We stared at things on the wall, the picture of George Washington and the sign.

DO NOT SPIT ON THE FLOOR
TO DO SO MAY SPREAD DISEASE

I used to stare at Little Ploog's hair, at the way it curled up around his cap, while the backs of all the other

95

men's heads were shaved. We tried *not* to stare at new people in town.

When we got old enough to be cool, we didn't open our boxes until the steel panel in the postmaster's window flew up, meaning the mail was all passed out. And if the noisy window had startled us, we didn't show it.

But when we were little, we weren't so cool. Everybody in the lobby knew when we got a letter from Aunt Betty. We showed off her drawings on the outside of the envelope and told them the margins of the letter would be filled with drawings, too. It would be typed on thin paper and tell us about all her escapades. Sometimes we didn't even wait for the rest of the mail before taking it home for our mother to open.

Nor were we cool those rare times when we were in the post office alone while the window was down, when we looked through the empty envelopes in the wastebasket, in case anybody had left money in one. That's probably why the town collection can for funeral flowers was kept in Hunt's store.

Forget about going through the wastebasket in the evening. Some people would be waiting in the lobby before the mail even came, with those expecting something important looking out that side window every two minutes. Then the truck would pull in and you couldn't see anything but a black strip reading PENNSYLVANIA RAILROAD running diagonally down the side of a red semi-trailer. We Spurlock girls didn't waste any time up there, though, because we could pick out the sound of that truck when it came around the south curve.

The writing stand in the middle of the post office lobby was the town show-and-tell booth. The most fascinating thing I ever saw on that ink-stained marble top was brought in, wrapped in waxed paper wrapped in paper towels, by Sandra Layman, a girl who delighted in shocking people.

After everybody in the lobby had crowded around, she slowly folded back the papers, one at a time, until we were looking right at it—a cow's eyeball! She had got it that day from her grandpa's farm, where he was butchering. I couldn't believe the size of that thing; it looked as big as a *baseball*. With our faces all twisted up, we stared at it from different angles until the mail was out.

The eyeball met its end the next day at school when it was run over repeatedly by a bicycle.

The Shaw Apartments

Two low buildings containing four apartments sat across Brown Street from the post office. These had been built by Edgar Shaw after the 1932 tornado wrecked the two-story brick buildings that had stood there for probably a hundred years. The wrecked corner building had housed Mr. Nauer's earlier drugstore downstairs and its upstairs was the place known as "Hengstler's Hall."

Vernon newlyweds usually started out in the Shaw apartments, which made it a good place to check out new-born babies when we got the mail. One of the prettiest babies we saw in there was Paul and Kate Carney's little Linda. We gave the baby our stamp of

ALLEN JAMES LOOKING INTO A SHAW APARTMENT

approval and said she could live in Vernon all her life if she wanted to.

Besides dirty-faced little girls breathing on their babies, the newlyweds had to contend with their neighbor Gladys Eitel coming into their apartments without knocking. And if she couldn't raise anybody, she searched the apartment until she did. Some newlyweds put hooks on their screen doors.

The plumbing in the Shaw apartments was always getting plugged up. Edgar Shaw blamed it on the fact that newlyweds lived there. He said newlyweds flushed things down the commodes other people didn't use so much.

Jordan's Funeral Home

A wonderful thing happened in 1946. Ralph Jordan moved his funeral home to our side of town, right across the highway, in fact, where Mr. Gannon used to live. Now we had another stop on our route to the post office, and in one trip could check out not only the new babies in Vernon, but also the people leaving.

The funeral home was like a mansion...thick carpeting, chandeliers, a curved stairway, the kind of place that made us whisper even when no one was around. Our mother took us over when they had their grand opening. Dorothy talked for days afterwards about the Queen Anne's lace Millie Jordan had dyed with colored chalk dust and put out in vases.

Lew Wallace, the man who wrote *Ben Hur,* had slept in this beautiful house while still alive. It was during the Civil War, when he was the youngest major general ever to serve in the United States Army. He'd come to Vernon with over a thousand militia prepared to meet the southern general John Hunt Morgan, who was raiding Indiana.

If a body was laid out in the funeral home, Katie and I inspected it during the morning hours, when no relatives would be there. Ralph Jordan and Martin Sandefur and

Frank Fisher didn't mind a bit when we stopped in. We *guessed* they didn't mind it; we never actually asked them. Katie, always braver than I, had to reach into the casket and touch every corpse. She wouldn't tell me how the bodies felt. "Feel it yourself," she would say.

Sometimes we went to the funeral home to see a body with our mother, when a lot of other people would be there, too. Mary Bolser, the lady the funeral home hired to fix hair, would always be sitting at the foot of the casket. She sat there and told everybody where she was when the person died.

The backyard of the funeral home was full of flowers that Martin Sandefur worked on every summer day. My favorites were the rows and rows of grape hyacinths that grew close to the stone wall along the sidewalk. When we went over there to take pictures, I wanted my picture taken by them. But we were usually put on the steps so we could all get into the viewfinder.

I did a terrible thing to Dorothy one night when she was baby-sitting in the apartment upstairs over the funeral home. I sneaked in the front door and started up the curved stairway, slowly, stomping my foot hard on each step. By the time I reached the top and Dorothy opened the apartment door, her eyes looked like Orphan Annie's.

J. W. Coombs was scared one evening when he delivered the newspaper to that apartment. He said there were three bodies in the funeral home, two downstairs and one upstairs, and no living person to be found. Ida Belle Fisher wasn't afraid of the funeral home, probably because her dad worked there. She did her homework in the funeral home sometimes because it was a nice, quiet place to study.

When we got older the funeral home became kind of a nuisance. Sometimes one of the men would come across the highway and ask us girls sitting on the filling station bench to turn down our radio. Apparently the funeral home men didn't think the mourners filing out the front door wanted to hear Frankie Laine cracking his whip and singing to his mule train. We later learned why they didn't like the noise, when our grandpa died and a loud speaker blared all three days from a medicine show at the Commons.

Living across from the funeral home, we knew when somebody had died because we saw the "dead wagon" go out. It was a black panel truck with tiny windows. We couldn't see inside when it came back. The black ambulance was used for emergencies and for funerals. If there was an emergency during a funeral, the person already dead was finished first.

By the 1950s, the funeral home wasn't taking very many bodies back to their homes for viewing, something about every family did when our mother was a girl. When she was in the third grade, she said, a lady who lived a block from Vernon school walked over and asked if the entire class could come and see her dead husband, laid out in their living room.

DOROTHY ON JORDAN'S WALL
'DEAD WAGON' IN BACKGROUND

So the third grade teacher paraded the kids over there and past the casket of a man they didn't know. It seems the lady had spent quite a bit of money laying him out, and wanted a lot of people to see the results.

The Courthouse

In spite of the many hours we spent in the courtyard, we seldom went into the courthouse. For one thing, it was kept locked now after business hours, which didn't seem fair because people just a few years older than we were had skated through the big hall in the evenings. And yet, the courthouse, like a castle, was too beautiful for just anybody to enter.

About the only time we went in there was to impress a girl from the country. With her in tow, we'd cut through the courthouse on our way to the other side of town. I always climbed the back steps wishing and hoping—wishing I had so much as a nickel on me, so I could impress her by getting "change" in the treasurer's office, and hoping that just this once the place wouldn't reek with the smell of rest room disinfectant.

"Are you sure we're allowed to do this?" the country girl would whisper.

"Sure!" I'd yell, the sound of my voice and marble-floor footsteps echoing up the hall. By the time I was halfway through the building I'd be so full of myself I would have to swagger over to one of the brass spittoons and spit part of myself out. This required standing with hands on hips and feet spread apart. Then I'd have to show her that I knew somebody who worked in the courthouse. Every few years it would be a different somebody.

In the early 1900s there was a skirmish over the courthouse. Some people—not from Vernon—thought that since North Vernon was now the bigger town, it should become the county seat. Meetings were held and heads got hot, until the shrill voice of a Vernonite cried out, "You can't move the county seat to North Vernon because the courthouse won't go through the Narries!" and that was the end of that.

The County Jail

Since Vernon had the courthouse, we also got to have the county jail. There were two jails, actually, an indoor jail and an outdoor jail.

The outdoor jail, called "the cage," was on the east side of the courthouse and we could see it from where we lived. Prisoners got to come out into the cage and get fresh air and sunshine. It was big and tall and black, its top and sides made of flat iron bars riveted together in both directions, leaving openings about six or eight inches square.

Neighborhood kids visited with the men in the cage and ran errands for them, usually to buy cigarettes and candy bars. Lois Whitcomb said when she was a girl she learned the words to "When You Wore a Tulip" by listening to a prisoner singing in the cage. We liked the cage. It was the nearest thing Vernon had to a zoo and we learned almost every species of jailbird. And when it was empty, the cage was great for climbing.

A man escaped from the cage once. He was skinny enough to crawl through a rectangular opening at the bottom where a section of iron bar was missing. His buddy was too fat to get out, so he had to stand and watch his friend get away and run across the railroad embankment, never to be seen again.

Frank Fisher, who lived across the street, had stood and watched the whole episode. He even had a rifle leaning against a tree in his front yard because he and Everett Bare had just finished shooting pigeons off the courthouse. "Why didn't you *do* something?" people later asked Frank Fisher. He said he was too fascinated with seeing if the man really could squeeze through that hole, and after the guy had struggled so hard and succeeded, he hated to halt him.

The indoor jail became a special place for us in 1947. After years of envying Donnie Layman because he could play with his friends on the swing factory lumber stacks without having to sneak in; and the Coombs boys, who could sit in their window over the drugstore and let the White Star bus drivers shine their spotlights on them when they came around the curve; and the Cartwright kids, who got to play in freshly-dug graves; and the trestle kids for having candy thrown out by the locomotive engineers, something wonderful happened. Hank James, my Aunt Naomi's husband, started his first term as county sheriff. Now we got to play house in the county jail.

Even though it sometimes smelled like pee, the jail was a great playhouse because it had cots in it and a nice cement floor that was good for skating. Our cousins, Allan and Denny, slept all night in there occasionally when it was empty. Of course, we couldn't play in the jail if a prisoner was there, but it was usually empty on weekdays. People didn't seem to do bad things on weekdays.

When the indoor jail was occupied, Allan and Denny visited with the men. One jailbird taught them how to make model airplanes and they soon had those things hanging down from the high, high ceilings in their upstairs bedroom. Allan and Denny hated to see that man leave when he was taken off to prison. Another prisoner was helpful; he repaired the lock on a door.

A North Vernon man who drank on weekends liked the county jail better than the city jail. Somebody said he liked the food better. He'd get down to Vernon some way

DENNY AND ALLAN JAMES AT THE COURTHOUSE PUMP

and ask Uncle Hank to lock him up "before the North Vernon cops get me."

One Saturday night he arrived when Hank was gone. "I can't lock you up," Naomi told him. So the man waited outside on the steps until Hank got home. Turns out he had escaped from the North Vernon jail and walked down the railroad.

In 1953 the new jail and sheriff's residence was finished, a separate building on the courtyard corner, and the cage was torn down. Our days of touching hands with jailbirds were over, but I was in high school now and interested in touching hands with other kinds of fellows.

NOTE: THE JAIL CAGE IS PICTURED ON PAGE 48, BETWEEN COURT-HOUSE AND CAR DOOR.

The Flour Mill

The old four-story mill up by the culvert, called "the roller mills" by adults, sold two brands of flour--Snowflake Flour and Family Flour. Some women swore by one brand while others swore by the other, even though everybody in Vernon knew they both came out of the same bin.

The rest of the Vernon housewives wouldn't buy either because everybody also knew about the big water bugs that lived in the mill. I guess they thought out-of-town mills didn't have any bugs. Some of the mill's neighbors said the sidewalks were black with them at night. Mary Hulse said she could actually hear the crackle of these bugs marching past her house, armies of them. They were thick inside the mill, said the Cartwright kids' grandpa, who worked there. He said the night shift men threw scoop shovels full of them into the furnace.

The milled flour was sifted through big sheets of finely-woven silk. Whenever this silk was replaced, Mr. Cartwright took the old sheets home and his wife made curtains out of them. During the war, when it was impossible to get *anything* made out of silk, the other women admired Mrs. Cartwright's silk curtains.

The mill wasn't always a mill. In Vernon's early days it was known throughout southern Indiana as the "Branham House," a combination tavern and depot, the state's first elevated terminal. Old pictures show a nice, steel stairway with a handrail leading down from the railroad track to the front door. Famous people stayed here, such as Henry Clay when he was touring America in 1852 with somebody named Kossuth.

In the early days, when the track ended at Vernon, the locomotive engines got onto a siding and drove right into the

THE CULVERT AND THE FLOUR MILL

105

back of the building, through an archway, then onto a turntable that revolved them around so they could head back to Madison. The opening was way too small, though, for the locomotive engines of my day.

It was Tom Semon's dad, Finley Semon, who turned the building into a mill after he bought it in 1902. He later sold it to Jake Swarthout and Jake was still running it when I was a little girl. He did give jobs to lots of Vernon boys and they seemed to like working for him. A man named Etham Stanley drove a load of cornmeal or cracked corn to Kentucky every week and came back with a load of coal. Mr. Beck fired the boiler for many years.

Jake had one employee who came to work drunk a lot. He always had a good excuse, it seemed. One morning he told Jake why he came in drunk so many times. "I've slept on the north side of too many barbed wire fences," he said. I don't think anybody ever figured out what that meant, but every one of us enjoyed picturing the scowl on Jake's face when he heard it.

When Lawrence Wolfinger bought the mill, Jake told him, "You'll never make any money if you give people a full measure." (This was just a block from Paul Hunt, who told his girls to give extra helpings to welfare people.) Mr. Wolfinger sprayed the bugs dead, cleaned up the mill, and made a nice apartment for his family on the second floor of the south end. And he did give everybody a full measure.

He ran the mill twenty-four hours a day, still using the original steam engine, which had come from a steamboat, probably one that ran on the Ohio River. A nice thing about the mill was that it always smelled like flour.

Lawrence Wolfinger had two daughters who kept a menagerie behind the mill—rabbits, ducks, chickens, guinea pigs, even several horses. They entered horse shows and put on out-of-town rodeos. Since the Wolfinger sisters didn't have a big brother, their neighbor, Leslie Engle, watched over them like an old hen.

The Swing Factory

Some people said the first porch swing in the United States was made at the Vernon Summer Furniture Company, owned by Mr. Cull up by the Narries. We didn't think that was true. We *knew* what David Alexander said wasn't true, that this was where the trim for Noah's ark was made.

VIRGINIA BOWERLY LOOKING BACK AT THE SWING FACTORY

Every day at supper we heard swing factory news. It seemed the men played lots of jokes on each other, most of them involving their dinner buckets. One day Daddy came home and said, "We now have a black man named White and a white man named Black."

Mr. White came to work one day and said he had on patent leather shoes. "Those ain't paten' leather shoes," somebody said.

"They are too," Mr. White said. "They're leather and they're pattin' the ground."

Another time Daddy told us the factory had received a letter from one of the big mail order catalogs. It said a customer had written questioning the strength of a Vernon lawn swing they featured in their catalog. So eight of the factory men piled into a lawn swing and had their picture taken to show how strong it was. To further prove their trust in the swings they built, they put it right on the railroad track.

The swing factory paid every two weeks, and when Daddy got paid, we got our payday nickels. Sometimes I saved mine until I had four, then I went down to the store and bought a jar of pickles, all my own, and hid it from my sisters. One time Daddy worked lots of overtime and brought home a check for a hundred dollars. He was proud of that paycheck, and we all gathered around and stared at it. Like most Vernon families, we thought God must look like Mr. Cull, who once gave a thousand dollars to an employee's family that needed it for a hospital bill. He did things like that, but in secret.

Daddy started working in the sewing room about the time Katie and I were old enough to walk up there. We'd go around in back and watch through an open window with an awning over it while he hemmed the sides of canvas for steamer chairs. If there was anything that smelled better than a new box of Crayolas, it was the swing factory. We liked to suck in deep breaths of the swing factory smell, which came from raw oak, canvas dyes, and vats of varnish. We could hear the pounding of hammers and whirring of saws, and see black belts of all sizes quivering and shaking in every direction, and hear the men yelling at each other. We heard loud singing, and Percy Bolden's whistling.

L. to R.: CARL CALLON, JIM DETRAZ, CLARENCE HUBBARD, DADDY, HOWARD BUCHANAN, ORVILLE "PEACHY" REDICKER, WILLIE DAY, AND IRVIN "BABE" PHILLIPS

108

We didn't stay very long because I didn't want to be there when the steam whistle blew. And I didn't want to run into Harold Layman, the boss of the place. He was a handsome man, but he always said, "Well, there's Dick Spurlock's boys," and I didn't like that. Harold Layman was an inventive man who had designed a way for the shavings to be blown directly into their bin instead of having to be shoveled.

O. M. CULL WHEN HE CAME
TO VERNON IN 1924

The bookkeeper was Miss Sampson, a lady who had worked there for years. She came from North Vernon in a taxi, or rode with courthouse workers. We knew lots of the men who worked at the swing factory. We knew Cab Hunt because he drove the truck that hauled shavings to the top of our hill and dumped them on Grandpa's property. We called that our "sawdust" pile and every kid in the neighborhood played on it.

Cab Hunt hauled the factory's oak scraps for firewood, too, for $2.50 a load. When he delivered up our hill, say to Laura Hess's, he would pick us up and let us ride on the wood pile, then he'd let us help him throw it through the woodshed window, then we could sweep out the truck. He was a very nice man. He had blond hair that stood straight up, like the straw of the broom that stood behind him in his truck.

MISS SAMPSON

We knew Bert Stout because he was the school janitor. He worked at the factory

109

in the summertime, sitting in an open doorway where he could reach into kegs of hardware, count out the right amount for a swing, put it into a bag, then tie it with heavy string. Kids could help him if they wanted to, not for pay, but for fun and conversation.

Some men lost fingers at the factory. After Skinny Walt lost a finger he teased kids with the short stub. He'd stick it in a nostril and say, "I bet you can't do this." Kids who didn't know about him would make their eyes water trying to stuff whole fingers into their noses.

One Saturday afternoon when I was about six, Daddy announced he was going to run up to the factory. Usually, anytime the Maxwell was starting to leave, every kid within hearing range piled in, but I was the only one around. Standing there in my summer play clothes and a pair of brown rubber boots, I begged him to let me go. He said I could if I knocked the mud off my boots.

I did that, then climbed into the back and sat straight up on the edge of the seat, right in the middle. Ignoring the brittle, old leather full of tiny cracks that curled up and scratched my legs, I pretended I was a rich girl. I was an only child and Daddy was my chauffeur...and the reason nobody else had a car like ours was because it was so *new*.

I waited in the car while Daddy was in the factory, then he circled around the depot. (All kinds of things had been shipped in and out of this depot, even people. In the early 1900s, before cars were invented, a sick person could be brought to this depot and put on a cot in a baggage car and ride to Indianapolis.) We started home, but he made an unexpected stop to say something to Harold Layman, who was raking his yard with his son, Donnie. Harold Layman lived beside the Methodist church and near the highway in a house that was beautiful, and his big yard always looked nice.

Layman's had bought this house from Mr. Wenzel, who had ordered it from Sears and Roebuck back before I was born. As hard as it was to believe, this entire house, down to the paint and nails,

LAYMANS' SEARS & ROEBUCK HOUSE

had arrived in boxcars and was unloaded at the depot we had just driven around. What the inside of this house looked like I could only imagine, easily picturing carpeting and a bathroom.

Daddy kept the engine running because Harold Layman came over to the car. Donnie Layman, who was a little older than I, stopped raking, too. We stared at each other while our dad's talked. I don't know what he was thinking, but I was thinking, "So this is what a boss's son looks like." Actually, he stared at me for only about five seconds and spent the rest of the time examining the Maxwell.

Suddenly the men were through talking and Daddy put his foot on the gas pedal and my head jerked back. To cover this, I went *all the way* back, pretending I had planned to, until only my feet were sticking up. Once I had got myself into this ungodly position, I didn't dare show my face again, so I stayed this way, with dried cakes of mud falling down into my face, until we were well around the middle curve.

Donnie Layman was to deny years later that the incident ever took place. He also would deny that while he stood there watching my muddy boots sticking up out of our Maxwell as it disappeared around the Rogers curve, he had whispered to himself: "Some day I'm going to marry that girl."

Tunnel Mill, one of our favorite places, was hardly there anymore. The four-story front wall with its window and door holes was still standing, and parts of the side walls that were connected to it. The tall chimney still stood nearby, separated from the crumbling stone walls because the wood parts of the mill had rotted away to nothingness.

BOB SHAW'S TUNNEL MILL MADE OF MATCHSTICKS

The older people in Vernon made sure we all knew the history of Tunnel Mill. They said it was built in 1824, engineered by John Vawter for grinding grain and making flour. It was powered by Muscatatuck River water that came through a tunnel in an isthmus (a word we learned in geography) over 300 feet wide. They said *one man* had made this tunnel through solid rock.

When the railroad came through Vernon, products from the mill were shipped everywhere from a storage depot in town. The mill was prosperous then, but by the 1890s it was pretty much obsolete. In 1897 a flood tore out the back wall of the mill and closed it down for good.

Tunnel Mill was more than a building that we saw only in old pictures and the scale model Bob Shaw had made out of matchsticks; the whole area was special. It was isolated and full of fossils and wild flowers, a place to walk barefooted on an endless floor of solid rock, or climb over the huge wall stones that had tumbled back into the hole they'd been cut out of. Water sometimes pooled in this hole, but most of the time it was dry, with just a little stream trickling in from the tunnel and making a nice sound. After a heavy rain, though, the tunnel wasn't big enough for all the water that came through and people rushed out there to see it churning out of the hole.

One of the best things about Tunnel Mill was getting there. If you were on a field trip with your class, Tunnel Mill was a good hike from the school. If you went there on a family outing, you could drive out almost all the way by turning off the blacktop onto a gravel road. A small corncrib sat in the "Y" here, even though there were no farmhouses nearby. I don't know who owned it, but everybody in the county called it "the corncrib." When you heard that "Billy and Betty were seen parked at the corncrib," you knew exactly where they were.

Newcomers had trouble with our directions. If we told a new preacher, for example, that he could find Tunnel Mill by going down Madge Jordan's hill, crossing Dryden's bridge, taking the Dog Farm Road, then turning left at the corncrib, he would *never* find Tunnel Mill.

The gravel lane that left the blacktop ended at the Baldwin Cemetery. Since there was enough room here for turning around, it was an even more popular lovers' lane than behind the corncrib. Sometimes on grade school field trips our teachers went ahead of us to cover things up. When we were in high school, we looked around for anything that might belong to a classmate so we could call attention to it. If we found a red bandanna handkerchief, we knew a carload of boys without dates had come back here with the handkerchief over the car's spotlight to make the parkers think they were the law.

The Baldwin Cemetery was started by Ebenezer Baldwin, the man who built and lived near Tunnel Mill. Baldwin Cemetery was on the left side of the lane and on top of a very high ridge covered with tall pine trees. I was always afraid to get too close to the edge when looking down at the river. Some of the tombstones here were so old we couldn't read them, yet there would be a few new graves with the names on those little funeral home signs.

I loved to walk around here because the pine trees smelled so good and moved their branches even when no other trees did. The ground here was covered with needles, layers and layers of them. They were so soft we couldn't hear our footsteps. The Baldwin Cemetery was one of the quietest places in the world. Every time we stopped there, one of us would say, "*This* is where I want to be buried," even though we could see the Vernon Cemetery right across the river.

Beginning here, we traveled on a descending path that was narrow and rocky and went through a dark woods with big grape vines hanging down to the ground. When we saw a brightness ahead, we knew we had reached our destination, Tunnel Mill.

The other route to Tunnel Mill—the shortcut—was the tunnel itself. "The opening's just across the river from the Vernon Cemetery," we'd tell new people. But strangers had trouble finding this, too, because a strip of horseweeds separated the mowed part of the cemetery from the sandy banks of the Muscatatuck. You almost had to be right even with that opening across the river to see it. First you had to find exactly the right path in the network of paths through those weeds. Once you found it, though, crossing the river was easy because the remains of the dam Mr. Baldwin built were still there. You never had to get more than knee-deep in the river and the water didn't swirl *too* fast around your legs. You just kept reminding yourself that every underwater rock was slick.

After mastering that feat, I practically held my breath through the entire 300 and some feet of the tunnel. I couldn't have done it without that small rectangle of light at the other end. It was shaped just like the tunnel, jagged-edged but flat on top, and looked a lot narrower than fifteen feet.

The tunnel was only about five feet high, so by the time we were teenagers, we had to go through stooped over. I always dreaded those ice-cold drops of water that landed on my back without warning, and I tried not to think about the huge slabs of fallen rock laying along my route. Still, Daddy's words always came back to me, the ones he would say when we were sitting at the supper table and heard a loud noise we knew wasn't the stone quarry or the proving ground. "There goes another slab of the tunnel falling down."

THE VERNON END OF THE TUNNEL

The cemetery was one of our favorite playgrounds. Even entering it seemed special because the cemetery road, a nice blacktopped road, took you to the top of the second ridge and the narrowest part of the hourglass. There you passed between the houses of two preachers. We thought the entrance to the Vernon Cemetery was probably what the gate to heaven looked like.

On the left side, beyond a sign that said THE MANSE, was the home of Rev. and Mrs. Tull—she called herself "Miz" Tull—and their daughter, Virginia Lee. Rev. Tull was the preacher at the Vernon Presbyterian Church, but he looked after everybody. One morning when the roads were slick and the temperature at $30°$ below zero, he walked out to the country to visit a family whose house had burned during the night.

All the boys wanted to date Virginia Tull and all the girls wanted to be Virginia Tull. She collected dolls and had twenty-six by the time she started high school. Dorothy said, "Ginny has shelf after shelf of dolls in her upstairs room." That room was so high she could see everything—Cartwrights walking out State Road 7, the spooners parked in the cemetery, trains, even the Keuthan and Patterson kids crossing the trestle.

Virginia Lee Tull wasn't a saint. She got into an egg fight on Brown Street one night. It seems she, Mary Grinstead, Bobbie Heaton, and a few other kids "borrowed" some eggs from Rose Duff's farm across Engle's bridge and allowed them to rot,

DAVID ALEXANDER AND VIRGINIA TULL

then threw them at each other until Rosie Arney called the sheriff. Mary said Rosie was out there at six o'clock the next morning inspecting cars and sidewalks.

Across the cemetery road from Tulls were Dan and Mary Simpson. He, too, was a Presbyterian preacher, old, almost retired, but still preaching at Graham. The church people hinted that his slender and pretty wife pampered herself a little too much. I loved their house, too, where Henry Ward Beecher had once been a guest. It's long front porch was held up by square pillars. I laughed when Virginia Tull said no matter what time she got home from a date, Mrs. Simpson would come out onto this porch and shake a rug.

After passing through this portal, we were greeted by all kinds of tombstones in the cemetery, lots of them big enough to hide behind while watching a distant funeral. The oldest ones dated back to the early 1800s. Some were great for climbing on, others for staring at, like the ones with little lambs and angels on them.

If we put our ears up to a certain tombstone near the shelter house that had a man's picture embedded in it, we could hear his watch ticking—some kids said it was his heartbeat. Kids taken down there by their big sisters could press their ears up against the front of the stone and the man would talk to them (while big sister was around in back). And everybody knew the big, box-shaped vaults down in the old part were haunted and the lids raised up by themselves at night.

In the daytime, the cemetery was a great place for taking picnics, and for playing with the Cartwright kids while their parents took care of the grounds. Except for a wide jump at the doorway, the shelter house was almost too easy for a game of "poisent floor" because the seat was one long bench that went all around the inside. Outside the shelter house was a water pump for drinking. We always had to get a drink, even though the water was warmish.

We knew where Cartwrights threw the old flowers from graves and that some flowers in the pile were still good enough to put back on graves, or to take to our mother.

When the cemetery started getting full of graves, the "broomsage" field up toward Tull's house was opened up by Dudley Childs, who must have been some kind of a big shot because Mr. Nauer ordered his Dutch Masters cigars by the boxful. Dudley Childs let us Vernon kids ride on the bulldozers with him and his men.

Well-worn paths followed the river all the way around the cemetery, as consistent as the lay of the land was inconsistent. On the cemetery side, water entering the loop rippled and pooled beneath high, rocky bluffs that tapered down to low, sandy beaches full of tiny shells. Then the bank rose back up to a high cliff again at the end of the loop. We just had every kind of river we wanted down at the cemetery.

Muscatatuck State Park

Every evening the sun set in the Muscatatuck State Park, which lay between Vernon and North Vernon. It contained acres and acres of deep, green woods with a blacktop road that wound all through it and ended at the big shelter house. There was a little shelter house, too, and either was good for parties. Both were filled with that burnt wood and roasted marshmallow smell.

The fire tower stood near the big shelter house. It tapered up to the sky, was made of steel, and had zigzag steps for climbing to a tiny house at the top. If you climbed halfway up the steps, you had to go all the way because there was always a wasp nest about halfway up and by that time they were riled.

Once at the top, you could knock on the trap door in the floor of the house and the man who worked there would open it and help you up. The top part of this house, which held only two or three people, was all glass. A map of the county covered a table in the middle, where lay a pair of binoculars we could use for looking down on treetops and over at Vernon.

THE FIRE TOWER

We couldn't go to the park by ourselves, but spent many an hour there with church and scout groups. My favorite trail began at the place I called "the castle," where stone steps curved down to a wooden bridge. The trail itself, the Vinegar Mill Trail, ran along the river and beneath gigantic boulders that had been washed out underneath and you could sit under them if it rained. I named one the "rock of ages" after a church song.

ALONG VINEGAR MILLS TRAIL
MUSCATATUCK STATE PARK, IND

119

A MAN SITTING ON THE ROCK OF AGES IN MUSCATATUCK PARK

━━━━━━━━━━━━━━

Things to Do with bugs

Watch for a fat bumblebee to crawl into a rose of Sharon blossom, then pinch the ends of the petals together so he can't get out. You can hear him buzzing in there, and feel the vibrations. Bumblebees really get mad when you do this, so get ready to run when you let go of the flower.

After dark find a giant pinching bug and tie a string on its leg and you have a pet. Do the same with a June bug. Do lots of June bugs and you can walk around with a bouquet of them, all buzzing around at the ends of their strings.

Find an empty jar at your grandma's house; grandmas never throw away empty jars. Punch holes in the lid, then catch some lightning bugs and you have a flashlight that doesn't cost anything.

Ball bugs were made to play with, that's why they roll up into balls. When you're done playing with them, they just walk away and you know they had as much fun as you did.

SIDEWALKS AND SILVER WHEELS

Growing up on tree-lined sidewalks is nice, but growing up on sidewalks lined with *maple* trees is rich. Maple trees have roots that stay close to the top of the ground, as if they're afraid they'll miss something. This makes for some of the best outdoor roller skating in the world because these roots do funny things to sidewalk squares.

They do all kinds of things. Without breaking some squares at all, these roots can tilt them in two directions. They can make a step where a step isn't supposed to be. Some roots break a square into fragments, every one leaning in a different direction, or all of them joining together to form a round bulge.

Where a maple root has been at work for many years, part of the concrete is gone and a patch of grass might be growing there. During school months I walked four times a day over one of these in front of the Heilman house. The grassy part was shaped like a little girl wearing a full skirt and a sunbonnet. Sometimes—when nobody was around—I spoke to her.

Vernon was so old some of her sidewalk squares had been replaced, but the replacement squares weren't all alike. Some new squares were white concrete as smooth as January ice—there was a double row of them in front of the Ale house. Others were white concrete, too, but with trowel marks all over them, while others didn't even look like concrete. They were brownish and made out of a lot of little rocks mixed together. These were called "aggravate." As nice as the new squares were, though, they didn't smell nearly as good after a summer shower as the old ones did.

With such an exciting course laid out for us, every Vernon girl had to own a pair of roller skates if she didn't own another store-bought toy. We could feel our little pulses beating every time we clamped those skates to the soles of our oxfords. (Skating was one of the few activities worth the sacrifice of putting on socks and shoes in the summer.) Our skates were silver-colored steel, made well enough to be passed down through the family.

Once we adjusted them to fit our shoes, we used a skate key to lock them in place. A skate key was not like any other key. One end was flat with a hexagon hole for lengthening the skates. The other end was a square for adjusting the steel clamps that curved up around the fronts of our shoes. Because we had to carry the key with us to tighten or remove the skates, there was a slot in it for slipping it onto the leather strap that went around our ankles. Most of us kept our keys hanging around our necks, on strings that were once white.

Katie and I usually skated together, starting our route with the courthouse square. The sidewalk there was better than the others in town and most of it was level. Here we could take those long, gliding warm-up strides...one foot, then the other. Our wheels clicked across the cracks like locomotives clicked over the rails when they slowed down for the depot.

KATIE HAMMING IT UP

The courthouse square also was a good place for speed skating, for leaning from side to side taking short, fast strokes until our keys were flying back and forth and bruising our shoulder blades. We liked to do this on the highway side to impress the drivers.

By now we were feeling tough, so it was time for other parts of town, for the Rogers curve, where the squares leaned in all directions and slanted up and around dangerously close to

122

the highway. The sidewalk at the Rogers curve was like a roller coaster, something we had seen in pictures.

VanGorden's hill was dangerous, too. Starting at Jackson's, it was a fast drop, with the highway waiting at the bottom beneath concrete steps. Sometimes we had to choose between a deliberate fall and skinned knees and elbows or flying out in front of a semi.

We knew every inch of those sidewalks. We knew when to get ready for a smooth square next to an aggravate square, and the fun contrast of sounds that came from our wheels when we hit one right after the other. We had no respect for any of Kilroy's chalk markings, any leftover hopscotch courts, or any hearts with initials in them. The longer we skated, the more brazen we got. We skated right over those dead flies in front of the pool room, mashed them flat, like pennies on the railroad track.

(But only a fool would hit a Front Street hocker while on skates. Thank goodness most of them were stained brown with tobacco and showed up ahead. It seemed they should have called them "hoikers." "Hoik," not "Hock," was the sound the men made before they'd spit.)

We skated fast past Harry Heid's house because we thought his name was Hairy Hide, and only a screen door right on the sidewalk separated us from his front room. Speeding here wasn't easy because he lived in that house at the culvert corner. But once we rounded the turn, there was Mrs. Heid's flower garden and sweet williams leaning out of that scalloped wire fence just so we could touch them.

Anybody who couldn't jump all the way over the girl in the sunbonnet was a fraidy cat. That place was one of many reasons we advised our little sisters and any new girls in town to stick with the courthouse square. We taught them to go downward on the square's one grade, the one on the jail corner. We showed them how to hold the left arm out and be ready to grab that streetlight post at the bottom and whirl right around the corner without even slowing down. "It makes your hand green, but it's worth it."

"After you leave the courthouse square, watch the big ramp at the Hemmings house; it's tricky."

We told them who would be sitting on their front porches at what time. "And if the Bolser sisters aren't on their porch, they soon will be; they go in and out all the time. They like kids. Alma is the one who wears men's clothes; Mary is the one whose picture's on the Mother's Oats box, and the one in the wheelchair is Pudie. She's a grown woman who plays with dolls because her mind isn't right. She likes to have company, but stand back a little or she'll pinch you.

Do you know where Granny Jones lives? She likes to visit, too. She has a tiny, little voice and sits in front of her house crocheting. Across the highway from her you might find Max Spencer sitting in front of his house playing a fiddle. Most of all, remember this: If Jake Swarthout is on his porch, just skate on by."

We told them which stores they could skate into, such as Hunt's and Cadby's, and which ones they could not skate into, such as Wenzel's and, of course, Nauer's Drugstore. "And stay away from that loose gravel in front of the beer joint."

"Oh, and skate *around* the brown spots on Front Street!"

TRAINS, TRACKS, AND TRESTLES

The trains some kids played with were called "Lionel," others were named "Marx," but the trains we played with were called "the Pennsylvania Railroad." Nobody ever wrote a song about the Pennsylvania Railroad, but we loved those locomotives that came through Vernon, even if they did belch out soot. When we went outside in the winter to gather snow for making ice cream, we just scraped off the top part that had all the black specks on it. Too bad our mothers couldn't do that in the summer with their white sheets that had hung on the line all day.

Boys, especially, played with the Pennsylvania Railroad. Forrest Sandefur, the Brandt boys, and probably a couple of Hemmings boys once found one of those little yellow handcars behind the swing factory after working hours. They lifted it onto the tracks, started pumping that handle up and down, and rode all the way to Grayford. Coming back into Vernon, they were seen by the town marshal, Casper Clendenning, who started to chase the handcar. He quit when he saw that Mr. Brandt was on it, too.

Every Vernon kid, at one time or another, knew the thrill of letting the train mash a coin on the track. I had a couple of coins I'd let the train run over, but I kept them hidden in my treasure box because I was afraid of being arrested for defacing government property. And I knew I could get in trouble with my parents for doing something so dangerous.

After coins, we graduated to crossed straight pins. They were really hard to do because the vibrations of the oncoming train would cause the top pin to roll off the bottom one. Margie Fry nearly scared Dorothy to death once when she stayed at the track and held her pins together on the rail until the train was almost on top of her. "Margie! Get back!" Dorothy kept yelling. "Let go!" The engineer probably was scared too, but Margie was really proud of the straight pin "X" she made that day.

Playing on the trestles was dangerous too. The most dangerous thing I did on the Commons trestle—I was scared to do *anything* on the second trestle because the cross ties were too far apart—was to walk on that beam by itself out at the side. I felt like the bravest person in the world until I learned that boys had ridden bicycles, even motorcycles, out there. When a train crossed the trestle, they'd lie belly-down on that beam, with their arms and legs wrapped around it, just to see how much it shook.

THE COMMONS TRESTLE

Boys were always doing crazy things on the trestle. They would cross it on the underneath side, which meant having to jump out and grab that first vertical beam. Sometimes they put rifle shells between the track and the steel plate and the shells would explode when the train passed over them. Mean boys dangled their little brothers off the trestle by ropes. The mother of the Keuthan girls, who lived

Right: SOUTHEAST END OF VERNON AS SEEN FROM TRESTLE - 1941

just on the other side, made her daughters come into the house when the boys were horsing around out there. "I don't want you to see anybody splatter on the rocks," she would say.

Every once in awhile a boy did fall off the trestle and was *very* sore for awhile. Good thing those Vernon boys were tough.

A PENNSYLVANIA RAILROAD WORK TRAIN

Another Little-Known Fact about Vernon

Henry J. Schnadinger bought Woodrow Swaggart's blacksmith shop at the corner of Jackson and Montgomery Streets for the material. After Henry and his son, Henry N., tore down the building, they hauled the throwaway parts to the bluff behind the schoolhouse in a wagon drawn by two horses. The horses backed the wagon too far and it went over. The two Henrys jumped to safety, but one of the horses was killed.

THE PEOPLE BEYOND THE TRESTLES

The Commons trestle was a crossing for people as well as for trains. Several families lived on the other side and walked back and forth across the top of it all the time. The rest of us held them in awe because of the dangers involved in their daily trips. Virginia Bowerly even had to cross the second trestle to get to her house.

I guess a person couldn't fall all the way through the first trestle, because about every girl who lived out there, and maybe the boys (if they'd ever admit it), had made a misstep and ended up with a badly skinned thigh. That happened very seldom, though; they usually walked across there day or night like the rest of us walked on a sidewalk. Without looking down they knew every space and tie, none of which seemed to be the same size, like we knew every crack and bulge in the sidewalks between us and the school.

In the winter, they said, snow blew in between the ties and the trestle *did* look like a sidewalk, one solid sheet. On warm spring days they expected to walk around snakes and lizards out there sunning themselves. Oncoming trains seemed to be the least of their annoyances. When asked, "What is the scariest thing about crossing the trestle?" they always answered, "lightning!" They said it wasn't so much that they felt like human lightning rods, but because they would be momentarily blinded and disoriented.

By the time these kids reached the trestle on Sundays after church, we were already home and had our clothes changed. If the leaves were off the trees, we could see them from our stairway window, tiny stick figures in colorful clothing, strung out across the top of the dull, black iron-work. Two here, one there, three on down toward the end, they decorated the trestle like candles on a cake. We could see the middle-sized kids break into a run about halfway across, and we could see occasional flashes of the white Sunday school papers the younger ones were carrying home to their mothers. Sundays after church definitely was the best time to stare at the trestle and think about those families.

The Keuthan-Hunt Family

My classmate Bernice Keuthan lived just across the first trestle. She had three older sisters, and when her father died, her mother remarried and had four more girls. They all waved at the train crews and at Christmas one year the engine stopped in front of their house and one of the men got off and gave them a basket of treats.

Their house was very close to the railroad track, in the triangle formed by the track and the two forks of the river. They couldn't get to their house by car, so they didn't own a car. Their paper box was in the Commons and their ice card on Bert Nauer's front porch. On hot days the girls had to watch for the ice man and get that ice off Nauer's porch and across the trestle as fast as they could.

Living near the track had its disadvantages. Tramps often stopped by their house. If their mother was home alone, she didn't unlock the door. A tramp once knocked on the door and asked for a straight pin and she pushed it through the screen. Maybe he wanted to make an "X" on the track.

I hardly ever saw Bernice's mother. Like a lot of Vernon mothers, she didn't get out of the house much. We never knew Mr. Keuthan, but we thought the Keuthan girls were lucky when their mother married Cab Hunt because he was that nice man who drove the swing factory trucks. On icy mornings he would leave for work carrying a bucket of ashes and sprinkle them on the trestle so it wouldn't be slick when the girls went to school.

Cab Hunt walked home for lunch, going straight down the railroad from the factory. He had made two carts as wide as the track for hauling things. One of them was for loads of a hundred pounds or less and he used it mainly for groceries. He had made it by fastening a roller skate on each end of a wide board, then putting big washers on the sides of the skate wheels to keep them on the rails.

His bigger cart had real track wheels on it that had come off an old railroad cart used for hauling cross ties. He transported about everything on it, and was never caught by a train. He had timed himself, though, and knew he could get it off the track in less than a minute.

BERNICE KEUTHAN AND FRIEND, DELLA YOUNG, WITH PATTERSON HOUSE IN BACKGROUND

Whenever his wife had given birth to a baby and was ready to come home—she always moved into town with a relative when due—Cab Hunt borrowed a car and brought her out to where the county road ended near the second trestle. He then put his best cart on the track, placed her and the new baby girl comfortably on it, and pulled them home on the rails.

Pattersons

Patterson's house sat on top of the hill to the left of the trestle and could be seen from town. It was a beautiful house that appeared to be on fire when the evening sun rays got under its front porch roof and reflected in the windows. What made this so startling to newcomers was that it happened long after the sun had quit shining anyplace in Vernon. If Patterson's house had really caught fire in the evening, nobody would have paid any attention.

Pattersons had three kids who walked the trestle all the time and so did their dad, Dan, even though their lane connected with the road coming into Vernon through the culvert. Mr. Patterson, nicknamed "Sleepy," walked to town to meet the White Star work bus driven by Crozier Phillips, a Vernon man who started at Madison and hauled men to Columbus factories. Dan Patterson, who worked the evening shift, was usually walking fast because he was running late.

He missed the bus often. When he did have to hitch a ride, he'd beat the bus to Columbus and laugh when it got there. Several times he missed his Vernon stop coming home and woke up around Dupont. Once he awoke and found himself alone in the dark bus parked in its little barn beside Bob Shaw's house. He had slouched down in the seat and Crozier Phillips didn't know he was there.

The youngest Patterson was Barbara, who came to our house to play with Mary Lou, but Mary Lou seldom went to Barbara's house because she wasn't allowed to cross the trestle. Patterson's collie crossed the trestle; he came to school in the mornings with Barbara, then was waiting for her when school was out, just like Lassie.

When Patterson's mother, Roxana, started teaching Sunday school at our church, we older Spurlock girls got to go to parties out there. I loved that house and wanted to own it. From the big front porch you could see a lot of Vernon.

The one son, John, took us all up to his room once, where he had model airplanes hanging from the ceiling by threads. He also kept a big jar full of "V" nickels that he dumped out on his bed in a big heap. We all gasped and ran our fingers through them.

His older sister, Mary Lou, had the best figure in Vernon and the boys were chasing her all over the house just to make her run. J. W. Coombs, who was my age, was chasing her, too, but he said he didn't know why.

Frank and Hazel Bowerly didn't walk the trestle very much. Living beyond the second trestle, they could reach their house by going out State Road 7 and turning down a lane. Their daughter Virginia, however, walked the railroad track often. She was a cousin to the Keuthan-Hunt girls and played with them all the time. She and Stella Keuthan were like sisters.

We saw Hazel Bowerly almost every day because she cooked at Welker's Lunch. She threw dishwater and slop out the back door, keeping that spot wet all the time. We could *always* find fishing worms there. Welker's is where we usually saw her husband, too. He walked stooped over because he'd broken his back carrying rocks up from the river to build a well. He didn't know his back was broken until it was too late to fix it.

When Virginia Bowerly was a baby, her mother always held her up to the glass in their door to watch the locomotives go by. She taught Virginia to wave at the men on the train.

HAZEL BOWERLY AWAY FROM VERNON

After Virginia was grown up and married to Danny Lucas and living in that same house, she still had a letter she'd received just before Christmas in 1930, when she was not quite two years old. The train stopped in front of their house that day and a man got off the engine and handed the letter to her mother, along with a wrapped gift, which was a doll. The letter was addressed to "The Little Baby at the Door." Here's what it said:

From a friend to baby. Please accept this little gift for the little one who is at the door almost every day to greet us as we pass by.

Having no children of my own, I hope that you will not feel offended for my trying to remember the little one at the door.

Trusting that I may remain your friend.

Yours respectfully,
A. E. Wade, brakeman
Madison local

Wishing you all a Merry Christmas.

Mr. Griessbach

His name was Otto Griessbach and he stopped by Cab Hunt's house from time to time to find out the day and the month. All year round he wore his pants tucked into his gum boots, and often had a soft leather cap on his head. With a walking stick in each hand, he looked just like Shirley Temple's grandpa in the Heidi movie, but Mr. Griessbach couldn't have played the part because he had a German accent. We kids respected him almost to the point of being afraid of him, maybe because he always stood so erect, as if somebody had just shouted, "Atten-*tion*!"

Before he moved out to a hillside between the trestles, he lived in the last house toward the Commons with his wife and tall, blond son named Norman. When Norman was a baby he would be properly dressed and set outside for awhile every day so he could breathe fresh air, 365 days a year. Every Saturday his mother pulled him in a wagon to the Seventh Day Adventist Church at North Vernon.

The Griessbachs didn't eat like the rest of us. Mr. Griessbach fixed his own food and sat in a room separate from the other two, never eating meat, only raw vegetables, sometimes with clabbered goat's milk on top for salad dressing. His wife made candy by grinding up raisins, dates, and nuts and pressing the mixture into a pan, then cutting it into squares.

Neighbor kids invited to join the Griessbachs for their raw vegetable lunches usually said no, but during school months when Mrs. Griessbach invited poor kids from the country to come

MR. GRIESSBACH IN HIS CORN PATCH AT THE COMMONS

down there for lunch, the raw vegetables got eaten. There were plenty of vegetables because Mr. Griessbach had a huge garden between his house and the river. When he worked in his garden on hot days he wore a straw kind of hat that looked like it came out of a rice paddy scene in a geography book.

Kids who couldn't pronounce Mr. Griessbach's name called him "the goat man" because he must have owned twenty-five goats, which he kept staked on chains in and around the Commons, and on the railroad banks. Some of them wore bells on their necks and they kept the entire area mowed. Once in awhile he drove them through town to some pasture on the other side and it was like seeing another geography book picture, this time of a village in Europe.

We kept our eyes on the big billy goats whenever we went to the Commons. Everybody knew they could get loose because sometimes the train had to stop to let one get off the track. (Those pointy things on the front of the engines were called "cow catchers," not "goat catchers.") That's why, when we sang "Bill Grogan's Goat" outside of school, we changed the words to "Mr. Griessbach's goat."

The Simpson family said Mr. Griessbach saved Rosie's life when she was a baby. They said she couldn't eat or drink *anything*. They'd tried everything and didn't know what to do when Mr. Griessbach knocked on the front door of their house behind the post office. He held out a jar of goat's milk. "Here," he said, "try this on your baby." How he knew about baby Rosie was a mystery, but the goat milk worked, and when the Simpsons moved to the country, they got some goats of their own. Sandefurs said Mr. Griessbach saved Kenneth's life the same way. And they said he often brought citrus fruit to their mother because she had arthritis.

The Keuthan girls said Mrs. Griessbach saved Stella's life. Stella was very sick with pneumonia and Mrs. Griessbach came over to the Keuthan house and asked Stella's mother if there was anything she could do. "The doctors said there's nothing that can be done," Mildred Keuthan said sadly.

"Fix a pan of hot water and a pan of ice water," Mrs. Griessbach said. She dipped a towel in one, wrung it out and put it on Stella's chest, then dipped it in the other pan and did the same thing. This went on for two or three hours, and Stella got well.

After Norman graduated from high school, Griessbachs sold their house to Buzz and Joyce Bowerly, bought their first car, and the wife and son went out west because Norman was smart and would have a brighter future there. Now Mr. Griessbach had no home.

He found a deserted house on a hillside owned by Pattersons, out between the two railroad trestles, and asked if he could live in it. Pattersons wanted to let him live there free, but he insisted on paying a small amount of rent. They set Mr. Griessbach up in housekeeping and Dan Patterson checked in on him every day.

Because Mr. Griessbach was very frugal, even though he received a small pension, nobody thought anything about it whenever he walked through town with a cloth sack over his shoulder. He was on his way to look behind Vernon and North Vernon stores for discarded vegetables to feed his animals. He was sometimes seen gathering wild cabbage along the railroad track, or buckets of fruit—he would ask people for their fallen fruit—or berries or nuts. Joyce

MR. GRIESSBACH'S HOME

Bowerly often looked out her kitchen window to see Mr. Griessbach standing in the scraggly little orchard he once owned. Sometimes she arrived home from work to find fruit carefully lined up on her back doorstep.

Norma Sallee, who lived upstairs in the Welker house at the top end of the Commons street, got used to finding Mr. Griessbach at her door holding a bucket of apples and berries mixed together. "Make pie?" he'd ask. She would bake him a pie and he'd pick it up while it was still warm. Norma enjoyed doing this because Mrs. Griessbach had been a big help to her when the Sallee babies were small.

The women on the Commons end of town sent Mr. Griessbach food every once in awhile, and knitted him warm things for Christmas. At school, when we fixed up bushel baskets full of Thanksgiving food, we always recruited strong boys to carry one across the trestle to Mr. Greissbach.

If you did something for him he was very strict about returning the favor, which meant you might get anything from a bag of vanilla wafers to delicious wild strawberries to a head of cabbage. Some women were hesitant to eat the cabbage.

Mr. Griessbach occasionally stopped at the Fisher house to read a German Bible Frank had bought at an auction sale. He sat down in their living room and read silently, or read it aloud to the Fisher kids, first in German, then translated to English. When Mary Lou Patterson was in college, he coached her with her German lessons. Mary Lou's professors were amazed. "Where did you learn to speak German like that?" they said. According to them, she was speaking German from the highlands.

My sister Dorothy was a little afraid of Mr. Griessbach when he made his few purchases in our store. Then, one day in 1952, he came into the store when the radio was playing "Auf Wiederseh'n Sweetheart" and Dorothy asked him how to spell Auf Wiederseh'n. Writing it on a piece of paper for her seemed to make him happy. They were friends from then on, and exchanged letters after Dorothy graduated and moved to Oklahoma.

When he got old, he attended the Seventh Day Adventist Church at North Vernon, riding there most of the time with the Hulses, who lived beyond the second trestle. One winter Saturday the ground was so slick with snow they took him home by way of Patterson's lane and a wheel got down in a chuckhole. Mary Hulse said Mr. Griessbach got a big kick out of watching the Hulses trying to get that car out of the hole, especially when Henry Hulse ended up weighting down the back by riding the rest of the way down the lane in the trunk.

Another neighbor, Virginia Lucas, looked out her window one night and saw that Mr. Griessbach's kerosene lamp wasn't burning. The absence of that small glow on the hillside was very noticeable. "Mr. Griessbach's house is dark!" she shouted. Danny Lucas pulled on his rubber boots so he could take the shortcut, which meant wading the river. Dreading what he might find at the cabin, he wended his way across, feeling with his feet for those familiar stepping stones. The moon was full, but its light didn't reach the bottom of the valley.

What he found was Mr. Griessbach sitting in the dark. "I'm just enjoying the moonlight," the old man said with a laugh. When he asked Danny Lucas why he had come and Danny told him, Mr. Griessbach, not ever wanting to cause his neighbors any inconvenience, pledged to light the lamp in his window every night.

He did that as long as he lived there, surely reminded every night when he lit the lamp that he was surrounded by people who loved him.

0━━0━━0━━0━━0━━0━━0━━0

Things to Do with Wild Flowers

Clover - Make chains from the white clover that can be found in any yard that needs mowed. The larger, pink clover found at the edges of town is good for sucking the honey out of every little spike.

Daisies - A daisy blossom makes a perfect fried egg for the playhouse kitchen. Then when you're finished with it, you can pull off the petals to see if somebody loves you.

Dandelions - Anybody can blow all the fuzz off one that's gone to seed, but skill is required to break off the head, split the hollow stem, then press a wet finger downward and make four perfect curls. (You have to know exactly when to pick them; they can be too dry.)

Queen Anne's lace - Put one piece of colored chalk in a paper sack and pound it with a hammer until the chalk has turned to dust. Stick one Queen Anne's lace flower upside down in the sack, close it tightly, and shake. Presto! You have a pastel flower. This is especially good if you make a bouquet of many colors. In water they last a long time.

Milkweeds - Break the seed pods open and free up all those millions of tiny parachutes. Watch the wind scatter them all over Vernon along with the dandelion fuzz.

Violets - Violets bloom just in time for May baskets.

Virginia Creeper - not really a flower, but a vine used for impressing little kids. Go behind the woodshed and tear off the two end leaves, leaving three. Come out and tell little kids it is poison ivy; then stick some in your mouth.

Trumpet flowers - put one of those curved, pointy blossoms on each finger and thumb, then scare the little kids with your witch's hands. You can reach the ones vining on that tree between Prof Jackson's house and the cemetery road.

Bluebells - You almost have to live near a river to have bluebells because they like wet, sandy places. In the spring you can find them all over Bluebell Island, which is at the end of that lane turning to the right when you get to the cemetery. Ochses own everything on that side of the road, but they don't care; school kids take field trips down there all the time.

The bluebells bloom before the water is warm enough for wading, but you'll find plenty of rocks, logs, and sandbars for stepping-stones to get you to the island. When you do get there, just lie on a sand mound beside a big patch of bluebells. Get down low enough that you can't see anything *but* bluebells. Stay on the island a long time. Nobody in the world will know you're there.

Honeysuckle - Walk up behind the Baptist Church where it grows on a fence and smell it and smell it and smell it, until a bumblebee runs you off.

THE FAMILIES DOWN BY THE COMMONS

The Ploogs Hartwell

All the Hartwell men had nicknames. There were Salty, Choke, Happy, Muggy, and Sawdust, to name a few, plus the more famous Old Ploog and Little Ploog. Salty got his name when he was camping with some other men and oversalted all the food because he was afraid he would be named the camp cook.

We were sure our mother knew where the nickname Ploog came from, but we couldn't talk her into telling us for a long time. When she did, she worded it carefully. "It's the sound made when a man hangs his backside over the edge of a well and empties his bowels." She regretted telling us right away because we practiced the rest of the day to get just the right echo when we pronounced it...and we never drank out of an open well again.

Old Ploog was George, who was married to Patsy, and Little Ploog was their son Willard, also known as "Sunshine." Some people in Vernon thought Willard was mildly retarded, but most thought he just didn't like to work. Even though he was middle-aged, his parents treated him like a baby.

They lived down by the Commons in a small house that was built after the 1932 tornado destroyed their first one. Willard's life was saved, it was said, when the tornado snatched him out of the kitchen and rolled him up in a living room rug, which must have been a great relief to his mother.

Both Ploogs spent a lot of time at the river, Old Ploog concentrating on catfish while Willard caught turtles. Knowing every rock in the Muscatatuck from the trestles to the cemetery, Old Ploog taught other men how to pull catfish out from under those rocks by using their hands and a hickory stick with a hook on the end of it. That's probably why he often had on rubber knee boots, and maybe how he earned his living. He didn't smell very good, but Dorothy

GEORGE AND PATSY HARTWELL

always ran out to hug his leg when she was a little girl. She said, "I don't care; I just hold my breath."

Patsy seldom left the house, which is probably why we saw the curtains part at every window when we walked around that corner. Usually, she had a baseball game blaring over the radio. Everybody in the Commons neighborhood knew she was a St. Louis Cardinals fan. They said when the Cards won a game, she danced around her kitchen and sang, "Waltz Me Around Again, Willie." Old Ploog said he hated to see the Cardinals lose because it meant beans for supper again.

Neighbors said she cooked beans twice a day anyway. She didn't cook them long enough, they said, and the beans were so hard they clinked when they hit the plate. Maybe that's why Willard had to walk up and down the railroad track so often. "It helps my bowels move," he said.

Even though Willard was called *Little* Ploog, he wasn't little. By the time I knew him, he was wider across the middle than his dad. He wore overalls and a soft cap that his hair curled up around in the back. He proposed to about every eligible lady in Vernon, saying he wanted to get married when his ship came in. Poor Willard didn't know that nothing bigger than a rowboat had come in on the Muscatatuck since 1830.

He paid for his cigarettes—which he smoked by lighting one off another—by picking up empty pop bottles around town, also by racking balls in the pool room. Willard was in the army for a little while, until he got an honorable discharge because of his asthma, then he worked at the swing factory a short time. During the Korean War he had a job at the proving ground. "I hate to see the war end," he said in our store one day. "I might lose my job."

He liked to drink as well as smoke, and often had to hold on to the streetlight post at the courtyard corner to get his balance while weaving his way home from the beer joint. I often wondered what all those slanted sidewalk squares looked like to Willard. Maybe they looked level. When my little brother Teddy was born at home in the wee small hours of the morning, Little Ploog was the only person around for Daddy to tell. "Hey, Willard," he yelled across the highway toward the streetlight, "I finally got me a boy!"

Willard became something of a folk hero the year he took on the Internal Revenue Service. Several people in town knew he'd been getting letters from them, each more threatening than the last. Finally Mark Rieser and Wilson Flack asked Willard how he was coming along with the IRS problem. "It's all taken care of," Willard said, looking like he'd just discovered the Ivory secret. "I sent the IRS a letter and told them that as far as I'm concerned, the matter is *closed.*"

He walked to North Vernon a lot. People driving to North Vernon would see him walking home, then on their return trip to Vernon, there would be Willard, walking back to North Vernon. Or, if rain was falling, his dad might be walking to meet him with an old black umbrella. Somebody saw his dad walking to meet him in a raincoat, then when he reached Willard, who was already soaked, he gave him the raincoat and soon they both were drenched.

Willard was the only person I knew who actually measured the courthouse against the Narries. They say Willard stepped off the Narries, then he stepped off the courthouse. And to think Aunt Betty had told us it was a fall off a wagon that made Willard the way he was.

Vernon was as much a part of Willard as he was of Vernon. He never went to church, but did attend a revival at the Baptist church one summer, sitting near the front. When the preacher said, "Everybody who wants to go to heaven raise your hand," Willard didn't raise his hand. "What about you, Willard, don't you want to go to heaven?" asked the man.

Willard answered, "Vernon's good enough for me."

The Dixons

Roy Dixon and his wife Amy lived near the Commons in a house that looked at the railroad embankment in the front and a yard full of dahlias and willow trees in the back. After Roy died, Amy was one of the Vernon widows we Spurlock girls carried fish and rabbits and squirrels to when our family had more than we could eat. She had bags under her eyes bigger than Fred Allen's, but her eyes were able to light up at whatever was wrapped in the newspaper, even if it hadn't been cleaned.

Amy Dixon had a regular route she took every morning to find out the latest news. She seemed to have trouble with her feet and always wore maroon felt house slippers with plaid tops. But if anything exciting happened in the Commons neighborhood, she was the proud leader of the pack on the way to investigate it. She loved funerals, never missed a one. Her entire garage was lined from top to bottom with funeral baskets she got from the cemetery dump and sold with her own dahlias in them.

Bill and Lou Dixon were Roy's brothers who lived with their sister in a small frame house a block over. If you missed the south curve, you drove down toward their house. None of them were married. After their sister died, we didn't know who did the cooking. We just knew that when Bill or Lou came into our store, Dorothy had to recite what the other one already had bought that day.

I didn't see Lou Dixon as often as I saw Bill. I did hear a story about how Lou Dixon and Bill Bowerly were fishing across from each other at the forks with big, long poles and got their lines tangled together. Each of them became excited because he thought he'd hooked a whopper. "They pert near pulled each other in," somebody said.

Bill, the darker complected, was the one we knew best. On his way home from the beer joint, he held onto the same courthouse corner streetlight post Little Ploog used. He wore a felt hat that wasn't as round on top as Ben Henry's. Bill's hat looked more like Dick Tracy's, only it was *old*. It was a brownish-gray color with little triangular-shaped nicks all around the brim.

He worked at the swing factory, also raised corn between the Commons and the river and raised tobacco in the bottom land behind their house, sometimes paying boys to set it for him. He paid Forrest Sandefur to pick up night crawlers. Forrest said Bill would set a can of those worms out in the summer sun until they *melted*, then he would rub the black, stinky result on his arthritic elbows. Bill tried to get Forrest to take some home to his mother, but Florence Sandefur wasn't interested in Bill Dixon's arthritis cure.

On hot summer days, Bill would walk up to Shotgun's to look at the big Pepsi thermometer on the front of the building. As soon as the guys at Shotgun's saw that tall and skinny figure walking up the Commons road—if Bill had worn a feather in his hat he would have looked like Big Chief Wahoo on stilts—they put into motion their Bill Dixon joke.

They took the thermometer off the wall and set it down into the ice water that filled the pop case. The mercury had plenty of time to go down because Bill Dixon operated on only two speeds—slow and stopped. While Bill was busy crossing the south curve, the guys at the station lifted out the thermometer, blotted it, and hung it back on the wall.

Bill would stand and frown at that thermometer for a long time, fanning himself with his old hat while the temperature climbed before his eyes, until it stopped on ninety-something. Then he would shake his head, pull his hat back on with both hands, and slowly walk home.

May Day

May Day lived in the next to the last house at the Commons with her husband, Simmie, who painted buildings. She was Ronnie and Larry Day's grandma and she had the prettiest name in town. There was even a holiday named after her, and when my friend Joyce and I passed out May baskets every year on May Day, we got a special kick out of putting one on May Day's door.

May Day liked to sit in a rocking chair on her wide front porch and listen to baseball games on the radio. The more exciting the game was, the harder she rocked. Sometimes she rocked all the way across her front porch and had to carry her chair back to where it belonged. During extra exciting games, May Day rocked across her front porch two, maybe three times.

Joyce and Buzz

Joyce and Buzz Bowerly lived in the very last house at the Commons that they bought from Griessbachs, and the river ran all around their backyard. They had nice things in their house because they didn't have any kids. Joyce, a neat housekeeper, laughed and said she had finally quit finding reminders on the second floor that Mr. Griessbach had stored hay up there for his goats.

Joyce and Buzz once helped my family play a joke on me. They sold Daddy their old radio-phonograph console when they bought a new one, and gave us some records because we'd never owned a player. When the men brought the console into our front room and plugged it in, I was

146

vacuuming the linoleum in the bedroom and couldn't hear a thing. Somebody put Les Paul and Mary Ford's "How High the Moon" on the turntable and jacked the volume up as high as it would go.

They said my eyes were as big as 78-rpms when I came out of that bedroom. I didn't know if it was the beat of my heart or the bass of the music, but the whole room seemed to be shaking.

HAROLD AND JOYCE BOWERLY

Joyce Bowerly was the first woman in Vernon to own a zigzag sewing machine and she was as generous with it as she was with everything else. When I was making my wedding dress on our old treadle machine, she let me come down to her house and finish the scallops on her machine, which was still brand new. I had a little trouble getting used to the quick response of the electric controls, but the dress must've turned out alright, because Don Layman's brown eyes got brighter when he saw me coming down the aisle.

Things to Do with Tame Flowers

You can't do a lot with tame flowers because they're usually guarded by some woman. But Nellie Stout will let you pick a few hollyhocks, which make great dolls. Use a toothpick to fasten a round, unopened bud to an upside down blossom. The green, cup-shaped part of the bud makes a nice hat on your little lady.

Apple blossoms - Stand under an apple tree when it's in bloom and listen to all the bees buzzing. It sounds like the tree left its motor running.

Peonies - Find one of those white peony bushes with ants all over the flowers. Swat a flower with your hand and watch the ants fly off. (This has to be done when the owner isn't looking out the window.)

Daffodils - pick one or two, stick them in ink, and watch their veins turn blue before your eyes.

Petunias - Get down on your knees and stick your nose in one, then inhale. The petals go right up into your nose holes.

Bleeding hearts - As soon as a spring shower ends, walk over to Nellie Stout's bleeding heart bush. The rain stays on the leaves a long time and looks like drops of silver.

Some flowers—roses, poppies, irises—just let you stand and stare at them; they don't need to do anything else.

Remember, *any* flower is good for taking to your mother, or putting on somebody's grave.

PEOPLE AROUND TOWN

Cartwrights

Those of us who lived along the route of the Lethia and Haskell Cartwright family could hear them laughing and talking long before they came into view. It seemed they shouldn't have been so happy, with such a hard day ahead of them. Lethia and Haskell both mowed grass and dug graves with shovels and did all the other things that made people call our cemetery the most beautiful cemetery in Indiana. Because they lived out beyond the "Y" off of State Road 3, they took turns pushing a white wicker baby buggy with two or three little ones in it, while the older kids held onto the sides.

Haskell Cartwright was a quiet man who listened more than he talked. In the 1920s he listened to a Civil War veteran named Hugh McNew talk about his captain dying in his arms at Murfreesboro, Tennessee. "The captain made me promise to be buried beside him," Mr. McNew said. Now Mr. Cartwright was mowing around the two stones that were side by side, the tall one belonging to the captain, George W. Kendrick, and the short one belonging to Hugh McNew, buried more than fifty years later. Both stones read *Company E, 82nd Regiment of Indiana.*

Lethia talked louder than Haskell, and was strong and tanned and wore men's clothes because she did men's work. She was always saying funny things. Everybody in Jennings County liked Lethia.

When Cartwright's named their seventh child Vernon Hill Cartwright, we thought it was in honor of all those trips their wicker baby buggy made up and down the Vernon hill, until Lethia told us the real story. She said she told Haskell, "If I have to have 'em, you have to name 'em."

"I don't know what to name him," Haskell said.

"Who does he look like?" Lethia asked.

149

"All the men in Vernon," said her husband with a laugh.

So they named him Vernon after all the men in Vernon and Hill because that was Lethia's family name.

The Cartwright kids and their cousins usually ended up in the top percent of their classes at Vernon School. Four more children were born into the family after Vernon Hill, but even as a mother with eleven children, Lethia never stopped working in the Vernon cemetery.

Ben Henry

His blue chambray shirts and bib overalls had been washed so many times they were faded almost white, just the opposite of his dark skin. But Ben Henry's old hat, floppy and rounded on the top, was beyond help.

Of all the nicknames in Vernon, Katie and I got to give Ben Henry his when we were little girls. It came about one evening when he was sitting outside the station by the steps with some other men and Katie and I sneaked up behind him and sprinkled tiny rocks down the outside of his shirt.

"What's that?" he said. "Is that skeeters on my back?" and he reached around and swatted his back. We thought we really had him fooled and kept doing it. From that day forward, we called one another "Skeeter." When we saw him walking to or from Welker's Lunch we ran down to shout, "Hi, Skeeter!" and he would say, "Well, there's those little Skeeters." The nickname never took hold throughout the town; he still said, "Hello, little Miss," to the other girls. Ben never had a nickname. Most people just called him "a gentleman."

Ben Henry wrote nice letters. If we'd ever left Vernon, we might have got a letter from him. When people moved away from Vernon, the first letter they got usually came from Ben.

Even though Ben lived across the street from my friend Cynthia, I saw his mother only a few times before she died. She wore a white bandanna on her head, and white aprons over long black dresses. She and Ben would get out in the street and play like children, laughing and throwing pebbles at each other. Ben got out in the middle of the street every Armistice Day, too, in his WW I uniform, with his doughboy helmet and his rifle, and fired off a few rounds while dancing a jig.

After his mother died, he ate dinner at Bolden's every Sunday. His neighbor women—Mrs. Crist, Janie Rogers, and others—occasionally took him plates of food when they cooked big meals. Mary Bolser started doing his laundry. He surely paid her. Ben always paid his way. He even owned a Model T Ford coupe, black with yellow wheels, that he kept in Charles Hartwell's garage. He had turned it into a cute little truck by removing the rumble seat and building in a wooden box-like bed for hauling his beagles.

Ben Henry earned his money by working for farmers, who said his slow, deliberate movements made him the best hand around when it came to horses. He worked for dairy farmers mostly, Ernest Ross, Bill Simpson, and Walter Powell. Not long before I was born there were rustlers working in Jennings County, so Mr. Powell had Ben hold his horses while he took pictures of them.

Ben went to the Jim Boggs farm at threshing time. During World

BEN HENRY HOLDING WALTER POWELL'S HORSES

BEN HENRY'S HOUSE

War II Bernadine Boggs always took her kids aside before everybody sat down to their big dinner table. She'd say, "Now, kids, you know sugar is rationed right now; don't take any dessert until the men have had theirs."

So little Charlie Bill was watching sadly when Ben took a second piece of pie one day. "Mr. Ben," he said, "the rest of us like pie, too." The Simpson kids also had stories about Ben Henry. They said he saved their dad's life when he took a pitchfork to an old bull that had Bill down in the manger.

Ben was the first black man most local children saw, but whether they screamed or just stared, he took their reactions in stride. He was tarring a roof at the Simpson farm when young Billy got hold of the tar brush and painted his little sister Margaret, "so she would look like Ben." The Boggs kids went the other direction; they scrubbed and scrubbed the backs of Ben's hands, trying to get the black off.

When Ben's curly whiskers got grey and he couldn't work as much, he still ate at Welker's and played pool at Froggie's. If there was no action in the poolroom, he could be seen sitting across the street on a courtyard bench, ready to tell a story to some child. Many of them thought he was Uncle Remus. He spent a lot of time puffing a long-stemmed pipe on his front porch. He sat on a rickety, squeaky, straight-backed armless chair that had a seat woven of grass. Neighbor kids sat on the porch with him sometimes, listening to his stories.

The Coombs family lived next door to Ben in his last years and he played croquet in their backyard. About the time J. W. and Donnie got home from school, Ben would be in his own backyard, talking to his fat dog, the last of his beagles. As soon as he saw the boys he would come over to the fence and say in that slow way of his, "You boys gonna get up a game of croquet this evening?"

Ben played croquet one-handed, but when his cataracts got worse he couldn't play very well even with both hands. The Coombs boys wrapped strips of white cloth around the wickets so he could see them better. Nobody thought anything about it; that's just how friends took care of friends in Vernon.

Bicycle Charlie

The only other Negro person in Vernon was also a single man. His name was Charlie Smith but we called him "Bicycle Charlie." We didn't call him that because of his handlebar mustache, but because that was his transportation—a bicycle. Being a small man, he had to lay the bicycle almost all the way over to get on it. He seldom rode it though; mostly he just pushed it around town.

The mustache was just one of the things that helped us identify Bicycle Charlie from a distance. One of his pant legs was always rolled up and the other one in place with a steel spring clip. Sometimes he'd have a row of rubber bands all the way up to his knee. He was extremely bow-legged and for some reason, whether he was walking his bicycle or riding it, he held his head way back and looked down his nose. Some people said it was because he refused to wear glasses.

Part of the time Charlie stayed with a niece out on Rock Rest Road, but when he stayed in Vernon, Jake Swarthout let him live in a storeroom up over the flour mill. He lugged that bicycle up the mill stairway at night, then back down the next morning.

Charlie could ride his bicycle everywhere, including on the railroad track. Even though kids liked to hear him whistle his bird imitations, they sometimes chased him down the street because his wobbly bicycle looked funny when he went fast. But Charlie had been a school teacher in his younger days and knew how to deal with mean kids. He carried a couple of Ignatz bricks in his bicycle bag to throw back at them.

The whole town worried about Charlie crossing the highway. He would ride that wobbly bicycle right out there without looking either way, and, as J. W. once said, "He can't hear thunder." But people two blocks away could hear; they could hear semi brakes hissing and car tires screeching and they shook their heads and said, "Charlie's crossing the highway." (This was before Jake Swarthout got old.)

Charlie did get hit once after riding out into traffic carrying a loaf of bread he'd just bought at Shaw's Grocery. When the dust cleared, Charlie was standing there on top of his crumpled bicycle holding one slice of bread in his hand. His next bicycle was a girl's bicycle, which he could get onto easier.

I had just graduated from high school when Ben Henry was lying dead in Jordan's Funeral Home. Sitting in our swing after I had gone over to see old Skeeter one last time, I thought about all the trips he had made down to Welker's Lunch. He'd laugh and yell over to the funeral home men, "Look at them vultures, just sittin' and waitin' for me."

Two minutes later I glanced up from my magazine to see Bicycle Charlie at the courtyard corner. He just stood there holding his bicycle, looking at the front door of the funeral home as if wondering whether he might go in. Pretty soon Martin Sandefur came out of the funeral home, crossed the street, and took him over.

Staring at the bicycle leaning on the streetlight post, I wondered what Bicycle Charlie had been thinking while he was standing there. I wondered if he was thinking that he was the last Negro person in Vernon.

Kirkhams

Sharon Kirkham was eight years old, she had no hair, and she was the youngest of several children whose mother recently had died. Her uncle, Charles Kirkham, and his wife, Opal, a Vernon couple who had no children of their own, wanted to adopt her. Local authorities, however, didn't want to let Sharon Kirkham come into our county. They were afraid because her county was having a ringworm epidemic and she was severely infected.

Finally Dr. Thayer said she could live in Vernon under the watchful eye of Mrs. Binford's blue light, and Sharon Kirkham was officially adopted—by the whole town. At first she was known around Vernon as the girl in the white turban, but in a very short time she became known as the girl who was always smiling. She brought a lot of sunshine into the Kirkham home and into our church. And being the only grandchild of Mr. and Mrs. Beck, she was the apple of their eyes.

Local doctors were concerned about the X ray treatments Sharon had undergone. They said she may never grow hair again. Sharon just laughed and said, "Then I'll wear a wig." She sat proudly in her turban when posing for school pictures. She didn't let it hold her back at all. After her problem was cured, Sharon Kirkham's hair did grow back and she led a healthy life all through grade school and was a cheerleader in junior high.

SHARON KIRKHAM WITH NEW HAIR AND NEW FAMILY:
GRANDPA AND GRANDMA BECK AND CHARLES AND OPAL

Charles Kirkham was a lineman at the proving ground and Opal was a teacher. Both had gone to school with our parents and graduated from Vernon. They lived in a small house next to Henry Hulse's garage. Charles said it was a strong house, with bricks laid between the studs for defense. He said the militia officers had been quartered there during Morgan's Raid.

Charles, who looked like the movie star George Raft, enjoyed funny stories. When I told him about Posey Barnes trying to get Vernon's speed limit raised, he said, "My brother John, who's crazier than I am, had the same problem with his motorcycle. When somebody tried to arrest him for speeding, he said, 'If I stay under ten miles an hour, my motorcycle keeps tipping over!'" Charles said his brother and Raymond Sandefur and Lowell Brooks got even with the town by riding their motorcycles across the steel beam out to the side of the railroad trestle.

When Sharon was thirteen, Charles and Opal noticed a change in her gait. She had developed a slight wobble, an

156

unsteadiness. They realized at church camp that she couldn't keep up with the other kids. The camp doctor suspected a brain tumor. After Sharon underwent several tests, Kirkhams were told she did not have a tumor, but a very rare nerve disease called *Marie's disease.*

Sharon became more and more unsteady, but she was determined to graduate. A neighbor and classmate, Roberta Wells, helped her on and off the bus as well as around school all day. By the time Sharon was a junior, she could no longer deal with the high steps on the bus, so another friend, Sonny Sullivan, drove her to and from school. With a big smile on her face, she was just able to walk up and receive her diploma in the Vernon gym in 1959.

Dalton Bolser

Dalton Bolser was Vernon's artist. He painted beautiful pictures of Vernon and the surrounding countryside, selling many of them to outsiders. His studio behind his house was a small, barn-like building. It was hard to heat and Dalton had to work in his coat sometimes.

DALTON BOLSER AT HIS EASEL

Mr. Bolser was very active in the Vernon Presbyterian Church. Whenever a child from that church got married, Dalton Bolser presented the couple with a painting...yet another reason for me to marry Donnie Layman.

Old Johnny Jones

We called him "Old Johnny Jones" because a young Johnny Jones lived in Vernon, too, but they weren't related. When you heard Old Johnny Jones mentioned, several things came to mind—his happy disposition, his ability to drive tenpenny nails, and his being...well, in his own words..."allergic to water."

If you worked in one of Vernon's grocery stores you thought of cheese. It seemed to be his main diet, and when he ordered it, he sounded just like Oliver Hardy:

One pound of pimento cheeze, pleeze.
One pound of longhorn cheeze, pleeze.
One pound of plain cheeze, pleeze.
One box of cottage cheeze, pleeze.

Then he would top it off by asking for two boxes of cheese crackers.

Yes, he was polite. When he found himself in a situation where he couldn't spit his chewing tobacco, he pulled out the bib of his overalls and spit down into that mysterious darkness seen only by himself.

Old Johnny Jones was a bachelor, a big man who lived in a house about the size of most people's living rooms. It was made of large, red bricks and was the last house on the right before you reached Dryden's bridge. The *Grit* and the *Saturday Evening Post* were delivered to that tiny house every week. Old Johnny Jones said he would have them even if he "couldn't buy bread." Behind that house his big garden ran all the way to the river. The Delos Fawcett family lived next door. Frances Fawcett accidentally hit him with her car once but it didn't hurt him.

The men called Old Johnny Jones a "rough carpenter," but we never thought of him as rough, even though he usually needed a shave. He was nice and generous. He bought candy bars for people for no reason, even adults. What we saw him doing most was cutting Vernon's horseweeds, swinging a big scythe with a smile on his face.

Because of his politeness he wore his shirt collar and sleeves buttoned year round, and a buttoned-up sweater or an overall jacket, even in the summer. But the smells still escaped, smells of used tobacco mixed with sweat. That's when he would stand at the post office window and say to Betty Willman, "Stinkin' hot day, isn't it?" and she would answer, "Yes, Johnny, it is."

When people did things for him, he thanked them. Dalton Bolser took him to the doctor once, then stopped by a few days later to see how he was doing. Dalton asked Johnny if his medicine was working and Johnny said he didn't know. "I'm going to wait and take it when I feel better," he said.

Anybody wading the river under Dryden's bridge who stumbled upon a gigantic pair of overalls weighted down with a rock knew whose they were. And everybody knew Old Johnny gave himself a bath in the river once a year—with his clothes on. (Some people said twice a year.)

CAB HUNT, LUKE ROBERSON, PAUL HUNT, GENE RAYBURN, OLD JOHNNY JONES, AND ROBERT "BUCK" WHITCOMB

159

I don't know of anybody who actually saw him taking this bath, but he told Lester and Teenie Walt once how he did it. He called it "killing two birds with one stone." He said, "I go down to the river with my clothes on, get wet, rub a bar of soap all over me and my clothes, then lay in the riffle till I'm rinsed off."

He did clean up for special occasions. He was said to look nice when he joined a load of Vernon people Paul Hunt took to the state fair in his school bus. Old Johnny wanted to see Indianapolis because he'd lived there in his younger days. Also, when he served as an election sheriff he always cleaned up and wore a white shirt and tie. For this reason, he was often asked to serve as an election sheriff.

Whenever men hired Old Johnny Jones to work for them, their wives always saw to it he got a good, hot meal—something besides *cheese*. This included Mrs. Grant, who still cooked as if for threshers when she and her husband retired to their little farm on St. Anne Road. Even when Old Johnny Jones was no longer able to help much, Mr. Grant would hire him, come get him, and take him out there. "I just like to have Old Johnny Jones around," he said.

Tom Semon

Tom Semon, a big, red-faced man known by the whole town even though he lived up near the north curve, told everybody he became a lawyer not to get other people out of trouble, but to get himself out of trouble. To the rest of the town, it seemed to be his wife, Flossie, who worked the hardest to keep him out of trouble. It's a good thing she didn't have any other children to take care of.

Whenever Tom was helped home from the beer joint, Flossie would always bawl out the person bringing Tom home instead of bawling out Tom. Some men got so they refused to take him home anymore. That was his biggest problem—drinking, but he was said to get completely drunk only when he was dressed in a suit. During the war he got to his jobs at the proving ground and at Camp Atterbury, both far into other counties, by using his thumb.

He had all kinds of ways to sneak booze into the house. When people would call about bringing their tax work and ask what he would charge, he'd whisper into the phone, "Just leave a pint of wine behind one of the trees in my side yard." Then, when he had finished with his tax work, he loudly said in front of Flossie, "No charge! No charge!" He had the North Vernon taxi drivers trained to stop in front of his house, raise the hood of the car, then hide a whiskey bottle in his yard.

Tom was sitting in the beer joint one day when a stranger came in and asked if anybody there could notarize a paper. "I can!" Tom yelled, but while signing his name, he realized he didn't have his state seal with him. "You got a half dollar?" he asked the man, and the man reached into his pocket and pulled out a fifty-cent piece. Tom laid that coin on the paper, whopped it once with his big fist, and the resulting impression came out looking as good as any state seal around.

I think Tom was an only child. When he was young his dad owned the flour mill and had money. According to somebody who was around back then, Tom Semon and Riley Whitcomb were in college at the same time, but Riley was working his way through while Tom's dad was paying all his expenses. Tom's dad thought college must be awfully expensive and asked Riley Whitcomb one day what it cost to attend college. Riley told him what his own expenses were and Tom's dad hit the ceiling because he had been sending about four times that much to Tom.

In spite of his weaknesses, Tom was called "one of the best abstractors in the business" and was known for giving extra nice Christmas presents to newspaper boys...and he *was* one of our more entertaining people.

The Town Marshal

No matter who the town marshal was, the kids didn't like him because one of his duties was the killing of stray dogs. That's about all Old Ploog did when he was marshal, but Casper Clendenning took the job more seriously. It wasn't unusual to see him chasing a car down the street on foot.

The adults liked a marshal who took the job seriously. They liked having Mr. Clendenning walking Vernon's streets at night wearing that long-barrelled pistol at his side, even though it weighed almost as much as he did. They liked seeing the badge shining on the front of his hat, one of those captain's hats with the wire around the inside of the top to stretch it out flat. And in the daytime he worked hard to keep their kids from hurting themselves. The only time the adults seemed not to like him was when he turned off their water because they didn't pay their water rent.

Vernon kids didn't appreciate Casper Clendenning at all. They thought he didn't want them to have fun. When he caught little Susie Rogers answering a dare by walking across the top beam of Engle's bridge, he made her get down and told her parents, "If there was a prison for kids, she'd be in it." He did put Paul Sandlin, Dickie Lunsford, and Butch Chadwick in the jail cage when he caught them shooting the window glass out of that little cupola on top of the flour mill. After they'd been in the cage for a couple of hours, he notified their parents.

He painted bands of tar around the tree trunks in the courthouse so kids couldn't climb them. The Collins boys got mad at him because he made them quit getting sap out of the maple trees in front of their house. "Those trees are on town property," Casper said.

"But we make syrup out of it," they said. The town marshal wouldn't back down, so they had to quit.

The harder Casper Clendenning worked at his job, the harder Vernon kids worked at bedeviling him. They believed he needed to chase them as much as they needed to chase him. High school boys would unscrew headlight bulbs in their cars and Casper would stop them for running on one light. They made their cars backfire so he'd think they were setting off firecrackers.

Up by the swing factory some boys rigged up an elaborate sling shot made out of an inner tube and could make cherry bombs go off right over his house. "Cap Gun Casper" they called him. (I use the pronoun "they"

CASPER CLENDENNING

because I didn't dare do a disrespectful thing to an authority figure that might get reported to my parents.)

Casper Clendenning lived down the hill from the culvert and the kids knew about what time he walked home at night. They'd go to the top of the culvert and wait for him. His silhouette was distinct, especially his hat. From the top of the culvert it looked like a tiny trampoline just begging for some small rocks to bounce off it.

As soon as he went under, they ran to the back side and got ready for him to come out so they could try to hit that small target. He never could catch them. By the time he got up those two-foot-thick steps, they would be out of sight and he wouldn't know if they went north or south. Charlona Ochs and Randie Lou Chadwick actually dumped a bucket of water on him, then ran into Randie's home in the Shaw apartments.

One time Casper tried to arrest Tom Semon for being drunk. Tom laid himself down on the ground and said, "Go ahead, arrest me." Well, Casper Clendenning couldn't begin to get Tom Semon up off the ground, so he eventually walked away. When he was out of sight, Tom got up, brushed himself off, and went home.

Casper played cards every week at an empty house called "the old Lauftis place" on Rock Rest Road, just past his house and on the other side of the bridge. Vernon sheriffs always played cards there. One night Casper was running late and the other men were waiting for him, but just as he was about to leave his house, some state excise police stopped by.

"Come with us," they said. "We're going to raid a card game out the road here. We've been told they've got beer in their refrigerator." The other card players weren't very happy with Casper when he walked in with all those state police.

Gladys Eitel

Gladys Eitel was a bubbly woman who lived across from the flour mill in a brick house the same shade of yellow as her hair. You could hear her laughing above any crowd and she made even the heaviest piano rock. But she toned herself down when she played the piano, or her squeaky violin, in the Presbyterian Church or at high school commencements. Presbyterians said she would leave church when Prof Jackson left, after the music part was over. She probably said to herself, "If he can do it, so can I."

Everyone still called her "Gladys Eitel" because her marriage to Mr. Stewart didn't last very long. She said the divorce was her fault because she slept all day while he was at work, then played the piano all night while he tried to sleep. He continued to look after her the rest of his life; he just couldn't live with her.

Gladys was no longer as slim as she was in the 1915 group picture taken on the steps of the Vernon Academy. She looked smug in that picture because she and another girl had just shocked everyone by coming to school with their hair bobbed. She and Tom Semon were always in the same pictures.

GLADYS EITEL

Even though Gladys was smart—she spoke several languages—girls who worked in Hunt's store said she would come huffing and puffing into the store and give them her list, then dump all her money on the counter and say, "Take what you need, Honey." She sent kids to the store to buy whole boxes of cookies for her little white dog, Scottie.

As was usually the case in Vernon, Gladys's neighbors looked after her. Mary Grinstead said Gladys came beating on the door of their Rat Row apartment every Friday night to watch Liberace. When she got older, the young husbands in the Shaw apartments drove her up the hill Sunday mornings and let her out in front of the Presbyterian Church. She especially liked to ride in Ted Collins' convertible.

I always liked to picture Gladys pounding her piano all night, while the water bugs from the mill came out and danced on the sidewalks.

Mildred Brown

Mildred Brown stole Vernon's heart in spite of having everything going against her. To begin with, she almost wasn't a Vernonite at all. She wasn't related to anybody in town and lived in Vernon only during the three years she attended the Presbyterian seminary at Louisville. (In Vernon years, that's not even long enough to earn a nickname.) She had been born on the other side of the world, in fact, to parents who were missionaries.

One of her greatest handicaps, something that usually caused newcomers to be held at arms length, was not talking like we did. She pronounced *tomato* without the long *a*, *either* as if it began with an *i*, *route* like it was something hanging off the bottom of a plant, and *wash* as if there were no *r* in the word. And she hadn't lived in the Ohio Valley long enough to get her sinuses clogged up, so she didn't have a twang. Her voice even went up and down when she talked, almost like singing.

Miss Brown touched the lives of about every child in town because all the Vernon churches came together for Vacation Bible School. We listened breathlessly to her stories during the opening and followed eagerly her instructions for making unique things at craft time. It was Miss Brown who taught us how to make papier mâché.

Mildred Brown's married sister, who was a missionary in Iran, wrote and asked Mildred to send her a pattern for a maternity dress. Mildred went to North Vernon to Tech's store, where two spinster sisters, Helen and Marie Tech, sold dry goods. Mildred and the Tech sisters, as they were known, hemmed and hawed around and finally picked out a maternity dress pattern.

The bigger obstacle, though, came when Mildred took the pattern to the Vernon post office to mail it to Iran. Because of Iran's primitive postal service, the pattern could not be sent in one envelope. To make matters worse, Tom Semon was filling in as postmaster. Hard as it is to picture, Mildred Brown and Tom Semon had to spread pieces of that pattern all over the back room of the post office and group them in separate envelopes. Being a lady, Mildred had to be careful not to use the words *maternity* or *pregnant* the whole time.

The next year, Mildred's sister came to visit Vernon. She and Mildred were sitting in a circle of Presbyterian people when Mildred introduced her. "That's your sister?" Tom yelled. "She's a little person. From the size of that pattern, I thought she was as big as Gladys!" Gladys Eitel was sitting right there, but she just laughed.

Skyline Bill

"Here comes Skyline Bill." We'd say it before he even got to town. We knew he was coming, on foot or riding his horse, because we could hear the traffic on the cement bridge slowing down to look at him.

Skyline still dressed the way he did for those Buffalo Bill look-alike contests and rodeos and stand-in movie roles out west...cowboy clothes, long white hair, and beard. If on foot, he'd be using a walking stick with a gold nugget for a handle. While he was holding up traffic, chances were he was carrying a fruit jar with who-knew-what in it, anything from a live copperhead to a petrified baby. By the time he rounded our curve, the usual swarm of kids already would be drawn about him. I was too old to be that impressed, but I did like to look at his rings. He wore one on *every* finger.

Kids loved to hear his stories about adventures out west, his friendship with Buffalo Bill, his stints as deputy sheriff and stage coach guard, not to mention membership in the Vigilantes of Last Chance Gulch. "Tell us about rounding up and branding wild horses...the prospectors...the bullet wound you got during a saloon fight...your trained animal show...hangings...Deadwood Gulch...boot hill cemetery." The list went on and on.

SKYLINE BILL RECEIVING
CONTEST PRIZE OUT WEST

He had been something called a skip tracer, too, and supposedly knew every cave and hiding place in the hills of Montana. He said he earned his name running horses near the Montana town of Skyline.

I often wondered why such an important and famous person of the Old West had chosen to finish his life in

Vernon. It didn't make sense at all until I started asking around. Turns out Skyline Bill had started in Vernon, came back from time to time over the years, and still had relatives in town. He owned the silver brick house in which I had spent many an hour playing with my cousins, and my daddy had once shipped him a hunting dog.

Skyline Bill wouldn't say where he was born, but he had narrowed it down to two answers: "Missoula, Montana, to a Flathead Indian woman who died when I was a little boy" or "south of Vernon." Local adults, who called Skyline Bill "a professional character among amateurs" or simply, "a windbag," said it was the second answer.

If he was born in Jennings County, his first trip to the West was made in 1897, when he "lit out in a boxcar." During one of his trips out there he still owned Vernon's old hotel. He left a top room bolted and locked and told his renters that *nobody* was to go in there. But the tornado of 1932 wasn't afraid of Skyline Bill and took the roof right off that corner. The door had to be forced open then, revealing a room full of antlers.

When he came back to Vernon for the last time and got off the bus at the drugstore, Mr. Welker was the first person he greeted. Karen Boggs was there and said Skyline made her grandpa Welker mad right off the bat, and Mr. Welker usually was a calm person. Karen said when Skyline told her grandpa what he'd been doing, Mr. Welker said, "Bill, you were a liar when you left and you're a bigger one when you come back. You're nothing but a telegraph operator."

Skyline settled down on his family property south of Vernon, out there where columns of cedar trees marched up and down the hills. He put up a sign that read, "Wigwam Hollow." The two-story frame house there, where the old timers said he was born, became a combination of living quarters and a museum that was open whenever Skyline was home.

It contained sixty years worth of souvenirs that included guns, pictures, books, saddles, lamps, powder horns, posters, Indian trinkets, a Buddha statue, and, for some reason, Vernon's first post office window. Vernon boys got a kick out of pointing out to each other their own initials on the arrowheads Skyline Bill "brought back from the West."

Some people said it was all junk, but others estimated his collection to be worth $5,000. I was never inside the house. Kids who were said there must have been 50 racks of antlers hanging from the ceilings and everything smelled musty. They said they saw silver dollars dropped on the floor in every room, sticking out from the edges of animal skin rugs.

Everybody knew Skyline Bill had his grave site marked off out there, and a tombstone already in place. A lot of people had seen it. But I never believed what they said after he died, that Skyline Bill and his horse were both buried at Wigwam Hollow, standing up.

The Bennetts

The first kid our daddy met when he moved to Jennings County from Indianapolis in 1917 was Ted Bennett, who lived nearby in the same Cherry Park neighborhood. They met on the Hinchman Bridge, each happy to find another little boy to play with. Before long they were chasing each other across the top beams of the bridge and trying to see how long they could hold onto a muddy pig, but not at the same time.

When we came into the picture, Ted lived and worked in Indianapolis, so we knew him as a visitor, a fast-talking visitor who seemed to be excited about life. Anyone could tell Ted Bennett never really left Vernon Township. When he came down from Indy, he stayed with his widowed dad, Ed, who still lived out at Cherry Park. Ted's brother, Rush, was there sometimes, too. He was a cook on the railroad and not married.

Their dad was a short man who wore an old army coat that went down to his ankles. Once in awhile Daddy drove out and visited with him even when the boys weren't home. We liked to jump in the Maxwell and ride out there with him in the summer and play along the river. There was a swimming hole just beyond Hinchman Bridge, then the river flowed shallowly over a solid bed of rock that was slick but a great place for finding little turtles and hair snakes.

A third Bennett brother, Perry, lived at the "Y" just across the cement bridge from Vernon and for many years played Santa Claus at our church. He and his wife Ethel owned that wonderful hill over there. We were allowed to

PERRY BENNETT   ETHEL BENNETT   ED BENNETT SITTING
                                              IN A STEAMER CHAIR

walk across the bridge occasionally and go up onto that hill, which we called, "Perry Bennett's Hill." We always knocked on their door first to see if it was okay, and to find out where the cows were because we were afraid of the cows. Bennetts had a big police dog named King who went with us sometimes. We could see a lot of Vernon from up there; we owned Vernon when we were on Perry Bennett's Hill.

Right: VERNON FROM PERRY BENNETT'S HILL — 1950

Ted's two daughters, Carolyn and Lura, visited Vernon once in awhile, and we visited them at Indianapolis a couple of times. Being in their neighborhood didn't seem like being in a city, but they had to go to a park to do things we did in Vernon. We went swimming at the pool in Garfield Park, even though Vernon girls just weren't at home in swimming pools. I sat on the edge and thought about the time a bunch of older Vernon girls went to a public pool for the first time, to Seymour in Johnny Heilman's old army truck, and one of them came out of the dressing room with her suit on backwards. It scooped down *way* too low in the front.

Ted's coming to Vernon became an event at our house when he started bringing Carolyn's and Lura's outgrown clothes. They were *nice* clothes, from Ayres and Block's and other department stores in the capital city. Our mother had to referee us girls when we tore into those boxes. In a way, Ted played Santa Claus, too, because his arrival with a box of clothes was almost as good as Christmas.

Staffords

Mr. and Mrs. Stafford (Wilbur and Della) lived in the beautiful brick house on the road behind the school. They'd lived in the Cherry Park neighborhood until their son, who was some kind of big shot at RCA, bought them this house with the winding stairway. Mr. Stafford agreed to move into town, but only if he could bring his white horse and his milk cow with him. He put Whitey and the cow in the small barn behind the house. Sometimes Mr. Stafford got all dressed up and rode Whitey to North Vernon.

The Stafford's own children were grown up, so they were very happy to have Katie and me visit them, but, following our mother's orders, we never went into the house. We didn't care; there was too much to do outside.

They had grapes we could pick, and white rabbits in cages. Mr. Stafford didn't have the heart to kill any rabbits, so he just kept building more cages. According to some people, Mr. Stafford didn't like to shovel manure either. They said that instead of cleaning out his barn when it got too deep for the barn door to swing, he just kept sawing off the bottom of the barn door.

Our main reason for going to their house was to ride Whitey, who lived in the fenced-in pasture that sloped down to the lane leading to Bluebell Island. I clung to that noble steed—I saw "noble steed" in a fairy tale once—and rode all over Vernon, and all over the hills surrounding Vernon, so swiftly my unbraided hair flowed straight back behind me. Whitey and I were flying so high our heads were in the clouds, we...

"My turn!" Katie would yell, and I'd open my eyes and see that Whitey hadn't moved two yards, that I was just sitting on his back while he grazed.

Katie and I were a little disappointed when we found out other Vernon kids got to ride Whitey, too. We'd thought he was our secret. Then we discovered something even more shocking: The Presbyterian kids got to have what they called "Whitey-Watermelon Parties" because the Staffords attended their church. They would gather on a hot summer day and Mr. Stafford would lead Whitey around the school yard with each child on the horse's back. Then they would all eat watermelon.

Mr. Nauer, in a surprising fit of mischief, once used some Vernon boys to play a joke on

MILDRED BROWN AND WILBUR STAFFORD AT N. VERNON CITY PARK

Mr. Stafford...or maybe he was using Mr. Stafford to get even with the Vernon boys who slapped his Coca-Cola sign, or phoned to ask if he had Prince Albert in a can. Whatever, he told the boys one Halloween night to go up to the Presbyterian Church and act like they were going to turn over the church outhouse. He knew Mr. Stafford would be hiding in the church basement with a loaded shotgun.

The boys did as instructed and, sure enough, a church basement window flew up and out came the barrel of a shotgun. The boys couldn't convince Mr. Stafford they had been sent by Mr. Nauer. They finally got Mr. Stafford to go down to the drugstore with them and Mr. Nauer confessed.

After Mrs. Stafford died, Mr. Stafford's children in Florida insisted that he move down there. He agreed to do it, but only if he could take his animals with him, which he did, and we never saw him or Whitey again.

Burt Eaton

Our grandma never said anything bad about anybody, so we were shocked when she made this announcement: "Burt Eaton wears the same clothes till they're rotten, then he puts more clothes on top of them." She always took his empty milk bottles to her kitchen in the back of the store as soon as he left. She washed those bottles before putting them with the others that were ready to be picked up by the milkman.

Burt Eaton didn't smell Muscatatuck Rivery, like Old Ploog, or tobaccoful, like Old Johnny Jones; he smelled sour, like his dirty milk bottles. When he came into our store Dorothy had no choice but to wait on him. Our store wasn't as big as Hunt's, where the girls all said, "Who's gonna wait on him?" until nice Lenora Hunt would volunteer.

Long before we knew him the poor man lost an eye when a cinder from a steam thresher blew into his face. His glass eye was always messy, something Vernon women blamed on the fact that he never had a wife to care for him.

Burt wore suits that had belonged to Judge Matthews and was never seen in town without a necktie. He apparently thought wearing a severely dirty necktie over his yellowed shirts was better than no necktie at all. His neighbors said he washed his clothes by hanging them outside on the line when rain clouds gathered. The strange thing about all this was that Burt Eaton had some money and was probably more educated than most of the people in Vernon. He played the piano beautifully, painted, and made classical music on two old violins he owned.

Besides seeing him in the store, we saw him when he came to tune our piano. This seemed to be the way he earned his living—and ate, because he always made it a point to be finishing up a piano right at supper time. In households all over Vernon, the whispered fights away from the table weren't about who would *get* to sit by Burt Eaton, but who would *have* to sit by Burt Eaton. Adults must not have noticed the smell. After he'd tune Patterson's piano, their mother would sit down and play a duet with him.

He lived someplace off of State Road 7 south, near the Sanders and Powell families. Mr. and Mrs. Sanders had a house full of pretty girls who would ride to town with Burt. They always came waving and honking around our curve on their way to North Vernon, the girls happy because

BURT EATON AND HIS NEW TRUCK

they had a ride, and the dashing bachelor Burt grinning like he had more women than he knew what to do with. He looked even prouder after he got his blue Chevy pickup.

Burt ate a lot of free meals at the Sanders house. Sometimes he stayed too long and the girls were forced to find country music on the radio dial to get him to leave. When he got too old to come to their house, they took food to his house and pleaded with him to move into a nursing home, but he refused.

Finally he moved to the nice Poor Farm our county had just built with Jefferson County on the line between us. It was on 7, not far from Burt's house. The first time the Sanders family went to visit him, he laughed and said, "They scrubbed tons of dirt off me." He was around ninety years old when he died.

HAZEL SANDEFUR, DOING THE KIND OF THING BIG GIRLS DID ON LAZY SUNDAY AFTERNOONS

THE OLD DUTCH CLEANSER WOMEN

A lot of us little girls were afraid of that woman on the Old Dutch Cleanser can. We were afraid of her because we couldn't see her face, and she was chasing us with a big stick. Margie Fry once dreamed about being on the upstairs sun porch of Beck's house, across the street from her Grandma Cartwright's, when she looked down and saw a whole yard *full* of Old Dutch Cleanser women. Even when Margie was in high school, she still remembered it. She said it was one of the scariest dreams she'd ever had.

Since we didn't know what the Old Dutch Cleanser woman's face looked like, we each assigned her identity to a woman in our neighborhood, usually one of the older ones who still wore long skirts.

Apparently there were always Old Dutch Cleanser women in Vernon. Our mothers and aunts remembered a lady they were afraid of who lived alone across from Ale's. She'd shake her cane at girls who skated past her house, even the Ale girls, whose mother sent a plate of food to this woman every evening and went over anytime she saw a white cloth hanging in the window.

All Old Dutch Cleanser women weren't grouchy, but all of them were mysterious.

Clara Harlow

To me, Clara Harlow, who lived in the little end of the Decker house across from my grandpa, was the Old Dutch Cleanser woman. She wore long black dresses and had a shriveled up body and a shriveled up voice and owned lots of cats. When she called across the street for somebody to go to the store for her, or one of the Roberson boys to carry in some coal, she sounded like the witches in the Walt Disney movies.

Talking to her through her screen door, we couldn't
see her face very well. It just seemed to be tiny, with black
circles around the eyes. We never saw her hair; it was
always covered up with a bandanna or some kind of dust
bonnet, just like the Old Dutch Cleanser woman.

Clara Harlow was like so many old women in
Vernon; they never came outside, and when we knocked on
their doors, they barely opened them, as if they thought we
wanted to see into their houses. Sometimes we had to get
almost down on our knees to see the insides of their houses.

Maggie Abbett

Mag-gie Ab-Bett
Sitting in her window,
Doesn't miss a thing,
Doesn't miss a thing.

Some people called the Vernon Methodist Church the
"Maggie Abbett Church." Maggie was a grim-faced old lady
who, they said, used to carry the stool home on Sundays so
nobody else could play the piano. She once told some
farmers that wearing clean overalls to church "wasn't good
enough." She believed it was a sin to have pleasure on
Sunday. That must have been why the Simpson girls had to
sit in her house like little ladies every Sunday afternoon.

It seemed that being named after an earth person was
the last thing a church did before closing its doors for good,
and the Vernon Methodist Church was no exception. Evelyn
Mathews was the only person to come to Sunday School on
the last day of Maggie Abbett's Church. Maggie hadn't built
the fire in the heating stove yet when she turned to Evelyn
and said, "Well, if this is all that's coming, you go to some
other church and I'm going home."

I wasn't familiar with her until I started walking up to
Cynthia's house, then I noticed that Maggie was *always*

178

sitting in her window in a rocking chair. She never smiled at me or waved back or anything. After awhile I just quit trying. Sometimes, if she wasn't rocking, I thought Maggie Abbett was dead and nobody knew it yet. That happened in Vernon once. A man who slept in a chair on his front porch all the time died in that chair and people walked past him half a day before anybody noticed.

MISS MAGGIE ABBETT

Maggie lived where Brown Street crossed Montgomery, the most beautiful intersection in Vernon. On every corner sat a two-story brick house a hundred years old. Maggie's had a large side yard enclosed in a wrought iron fence that kept her apple trees just out of reach. She chose to watch those apples rot on the ground before letting anybody go in and gather some. And if she saw you trying to work an apple over to the fence with a stick, she pecked on her window.

I felt sorry for the girls in her neighborhood because she watched them constantly. One of the neighborhood girls, Carol Kingen, said they'd play in a place where Maggie would have to strain to see them. Then they would move just a little farther to the side, so Maggie would have to stand up to see what they were doing.

Maybe Maggie's having taken part in the first all-women jury trial in Indiana in 1921 went to her head. According to a booklet Vernon's Clionian Society put out in 1938 that pictured the women in front of the courthouse, it may have been the first all-women jury in the United States.

Cynthia's brother's wife, Mary, had grown up in Vernon and said she used to practice for church programs at Maggie Abbett's just like we did at Mrs. Welker's. She said Maggie's house always smelled like creosote, or whatever it was the Abbetts used on termites. Mary said Maggie crushed her one year by saying, "If you would quit glancing in the mirror and pay more attention to practice, you'd learn your part better."

Maggie once attended a wedding reception in the beautiful old Vawter mansion behind the swing factory and unknowingly drank some spiked punch. She liked it so well she asked for a refill. People who were there said by the time she left the party, Maggie Abbett was feeling very happy.

She faithfully minded her window post for many years. Having never married or had children of her own, she was able to perform a neighborhood service by keeping mothers posted on the activities of their daughters. But even when she clucked about everybody else's behavior, nobody ever told Maggie Abbett she once made a fool of herself at a wedding reception.

Katie Wenzel

Katie Wenzel was also an unmarried lady and had been one of Vernon's nicest dressers. We were told she wore beautiful suits and stylish hats, all "properly accessorized," and young women looked to her for fashion do's and don't's. She even dressed up and put on a hat just to walk to the post office. She had been one of the most popular girls in the old Hengstler Hall, according to Lois Whitcomb, and young men lined up to dance with her.

By the time we knew her, she was the strange old lady who lived in a musty-smelling house across Brown street from Maggie Abbett. In our time she didn't come to the door in suits or hats. She came to the door with reddish, uncombed hair flopping down over the collar of a ragged, faded housecoat. Her neighbors often went out in the middle of the night to retrieve Katie Wenzel from her wanderings and take her back home and put her to bed.

I often wondered why Katie Wenzel and all the other old spinsters and widows in Vernon didn't live together in one house. Instead, each one seemed to live in a single room of a huge house. It didn't seem...right...after dark, to walk past a house with thirty windows and only one of them lit up, and dimly, at that.

Katie Wenzel had gone further than most of the old ladies; she had taped newspapers inside almost every window. She seemed very afraid, and had furniture pushed up against her windows, too. The only people she would let in were her neighbors, Eva Stagman's daughters, who called her "Aunt Katie." They took her food.

She finally found peace in 1953 and Bob Shaw bought her place. After he'd ripped the newspapers down and fixed the house up, he sold it to Dale and Joan Bentz. Suddenly that whole corner was different. A swing set and sand box appeared in Katie Wenzel's backyard. Smells of full meals drifted from Katie Wenzel's kitchen. Talking and music and light came from every window of Katie Wenzel's house.

I liked those changes the Bentzes made in the place, but it would always be Katie Wenzel's house.

Cora B. T. Hargesheimer

In Margie Fry's neighborhood, the Old Dutch Cleanser woman was Mrs. Hargesheimer, who *shouldn't* have been scary because she was hardly taller than we were. But she not only wore a long black dress; she wore a black cape, a black hat, and lots of Indian jewelry. She even had black eyes, and warts on her chin with long, long hairs growing out of them. Her eyeglasses were held together with a little safety pin. She smelled dusty, Margie said, when you had to kiss her.

The men called her "Cory XYZ Hargesheimer" because she had too many initials and was particular about having her name spelled right. They probably wouldn't have done that if she hadn't been their grade school teacher in the 1920s. They still bragged about the time she caught some of them misbehaving at the drinking fountain. "Were you boys swearing?" she asked them.

"No, Ma'am," one answered, "we's just cussin'." Another said she once grabbed a boy by the collar and shook him so hard his shirt buttons flew all over the room.

Our mothers remembered her earlier years in different ways. Some said she was a "rough" teacher while others said she did a lot to help Vernon girls improve themselves and further their educations, the same thing they said about Harriet McKinney and Katie Wenzel. Aunt Vonda said Mrs. Hargesheimer told her she had artistic talent and encouraged her to paint pictures, but Vonda was still putting it off.

Cory Hargesheimer lived in a huge house inside the north curve that had sat unpainted for years, giving the weatherboarding a gray, spooky cast. According to legend, some silver-tongued man had come to town and talked her into building that house. The two of them were to operate it as a hotel and filling station, but when she ran out of money before the house was finished, he left. Renters in the house sometimes found her sitting alone in a corner of the dark cellar. "All you could see were her eyes shining like cat eyes," one of them said.

MRS. HARGESHEIMER'S HOUSE WITH DONNIE AND SANDRA LAYMAN IN FOREGROUND

Mrs. Hargesheimer was noted for canning raw eggs, an operation that began with a strange ritual Virginia Tull observed from her upstairs window. Every morning and evening the old lady in black came to the manse property, to a little red shed where she kept chickens. She stayed in the shed for awhile, then came out and went on her way. Nobody knew what she did while she was in the shed, except, perhaps, talk to her chickens, but the imagination did soar.

After years of staring bug-eyed at her haunted house from a safe distance across the street, I became friends with Della Young, whose family had moved into one of the apartments after Mrs. Hargesheimer died. The first time I visited Della, I nervously walked under the rickety front porch roof that had been meant to cover the gas pumps, into the front opening that never got a door on it, and down the dark hallway. To my surprise and relief, the Young apartment was a different world. It was probably the nicest apartment in Vernon and I was never again afraid of that house...or of any Old Dutch Cleanser woman.

·0·◖0◗·0◗·0◗·0◗·0◗·0◗·0◗·

Things to Do with People's Junk

If you've lived in Vernon very long, you know where every family dumps its junk and what you'll find there. The worst looking dumps are the hardest to get to, but have the best stuff in them.

Bottles are what to look for. Put the colored bottles in one of those heavy cloth sacks your mother's sugar comes in, then lay it on a rock and hit it with a hammer. When you open it, you will have handfuls of colorful jewels for your treasure box. A colored bottle that's whole when you find it might be too pretty to break up; it might be meant only for holding up to the sun and looking through.

Wash out the clear bottles and make your own laboratory for mixing up all kinds of concoctions.

183

THE SOUTH CURVE

MARY CALVERT

HALLOWEEN PRANK

DOROTHY WITH BETTY ARNEY

FEUDIN', FUSSIN', AN' FIGHTIN'

I was glad to be a girl, so I wouldn't have to get into fistfights. Yet I saw very few fights, even though every boy in Vernon thought he was Joe Palooka right out of the funny papers. Mostly, two boys would stand under a streetlight at night holding their fists up, frozen like statues and glaring into each other's eyes, while the kids all around them waited for something that never happened. I was always relieved, but acted disappointed.

The children in one Vernon family consisted of a boy, Donnie—whose nose never stopped running—and a younger girl, Ruth. Ruth was the fighter. When threatened by a bully, Donnie would go get Ruth and she would be the statue while he stood on the sidelines saying, "Sock 'im, Rufie. Sock 'im."

Most of the time, girls fought with words. I must have been bad about that because Daddy told me more than once that I'd argue with Jesus Christ. Of course, I didn't agree with that, nor was it true that my mother had a hard time delivering me because I was born with my hands on my hips.

When we Spurlock girls weren't *playing* with the Barnes girls, who lived in the rental end of Nellie Stout's house, we were having our best fights with them. Three Spurlock girls would stand on one side of the street and three Barnes girls on the other and we'd hurl mean words at each other.

"Tattletale, Tattletale, hangin' on a bull's tail!"
"It pays to be ignorant!"
"Come one step closer and I'll slap your face!"
"Everybody in your family has lice!"

Katie and I modeled ourselves after the Katzenjammer Kids, mean ones in the funny papers who spoke with German

KITTY AND CATTY,
NICE TO EACH OTHER

accents and made life miserable for "der inspector."

But while we made life miserable for our brothers and sisters and neighbors, we never fought with each other. We even came up with a pact that wouldn't allow us to get into a fight.

When it looked like a fight was coming on, one of us would say, "Remember we was gonna be..." and the other *had* to answer, usually reluctantly and with slumped shoulders because we loved a good fight, "nice to each other."

Health Tip

If anybody in your family has lice, bring a sheep into your house. The lice will go from the human to the sheep, then they won't be able to get out of the wool and will leave with the sheep.

WAR COMES TO VERNON

Early Wars

The war I knew was World War II, but war had come to Vernon before. When Irish immigrants were building the railroad, the Corkonian and Fardown clans fought all the way up from Madison, until a Corkonian was killed in a free-for-all between the two trestles. Afterwards a posse looked in all the houses where railroad workers boarded and arrested the ones with blood on their clothes.

When the Fardowns found out some of their men were in the Vernon jail, they threatened to spring their brothers and burn the town. They gathered and marched all night toward Vernon, from as far as Madison, and found the Vernon men waiting at the river. "First Fardown sets foot in the creek's a dead Fardown!" yelled a Vernonite. And that was the end of that.

Vernon was pretty peaceful then, until the Civil War had been going on for awhile and a southern general named John Hunt Morgan saw that his side was losing. He called his officers into his tent, where he had a map laid out on the table. "Gentlemen," he said, "we're not leaving this war empty-handed; we're going to march up to the North and pluck the most prized jewel out of the Yankee crown. We're going to take Vernon, Indiana."

In July of 1863 Morgan was approaching Vernon from the southern part of the county with over 2000 men, having already looted farms and towns in what was being called, "Morgan's Raid." Vernon was getting ready for him, though few healthy men were still at home. A furloughed soldier rolled the town's one cannon, a gift from the Mexican War, up the hill and into a backyard, smashing a tin bucket of silverware buried for safekeeping half an hour before.

On this high ground near the Baptist Church the cannon covered the Paris ford while stove pipes and bronze painted logs sat propped up along the river. General Lew

Wallace with 1100 militia, joined by the few Vernon men, camped all over the south end of town that night, guarding especially the railroad trestles. No one in Vernon was allowed to light a lamp or campfire.

Michigan sharpshooters arrived the next afternoon, about an hour before Morgan. By sunset the opposing armies faced one another at the river. Then a gruff voice from the Vernon side rang out: "First rebel sets foot in the creek's a dead reb!" and that was the end of that—until Jessamyn's Raid, when Jessamyn West came to Jennings County to research a book she would call *Friendly Persuasion*.

Another reminder of Morgan's Raid were the two confederate tombstones at the edge of town that a southern group came up every year and shot a gun salute over. When the original stones got old, they replaced them. The new stones were inscribed exactly as the old ones.

The deaths of these two men were always surrounded by mystery. All the legends have them killed in a skirmish out at Tunnel Mill, but a handwritten manuscript my grandpa found in the old Sanford Tavern says they were scouts that were hanged from an oak tree near where they were buried. It said three scouts were caught, but the third was forced to watch the hanging, then sent back to warn Morgan. This must have been the truth and the Vernon people weren't too proud of it.

World War II

World War II was scary and real, not just a legend or an item in the old newspapers at the courthouse. I think the worst part were the blackouts, just like during the time of Morgan's Raid. Suddenly, after dark, the fire siren would go off and every house had to turn off its lights so the enemy couldn't see Vernon and bomb us.

One blackout happened when Aunt Alberta had just picked up Katie and me to stay with her while Mary Lou was being born. We were approaching the cement bridge when the siren went off and Uncle Johnny had to pull over and turn off his headlights. Katie and I huddled on the floor of the back seat and cried, waiting for those bombs while Alberta and Johnny kept reminding us it was just a test and our Daddy was one of the wardens.

The kids out by Crosley's place had to contend with Old Johnny Jones, who at that time lived in a cabin with a dirt floor. They said he wouldn't blow out his kerosene lamp during blackouts and they were sure he was going to get the whole neighborhood bombed. It seemed the only people who liked blackouts were daters, who got a kick out of having a law officer *order* them to pull to the side of the road and turn off their lights.

Some Vernon kids ran through their houses turning off the lamps because they'd heard that American planes flew over towns during blackouts and dropped bags of lime on houses where lights showed. These kids preferred to have bruises on their shins when the sun came up rather than embarrassing white scars on their houses.

189

Even the grown-ups seemed extra nervous. Any man with a mustache was suspect, and Griessbachs were watched twenty-four hours a day. Eyebrows shot up every time Mrs. Griessbach walked to the post office with her weekly package to Germany. There was talk that they might be German spies, and their neighbors said the FBI had called on them. The sheriff got a phone call one night when somebody sitting in a car at the Commons was testing his spotlight.

Then, just about the time everybody was jumpy anyway, Dale Cooper, a friend of Daddy's, would buzz the courthouse in a B-17. The town would get all stirred up, but at our house we just laughed because we knew who it was, and Katie and I teased Dorothy because she was in love with him.

Hitler replaced the bear who lived under the high, double bed Katie and I shared, waiting there at bedtime to grab our little ankles. But we foiled him. We ran toward that bed every night yelling, "Hitler's under the bed!" and our feet left the linoleum about five feet out.

Going to sleep at night wasn't as easy as it used to be. The proving ground way down on the county line never stopped booming, while men broadcasting news on the radio talked loud and fast. They all drowned out the swishes on the bridge and the squeaks of the rocking chair.

With the covers pulled up tightly around my pigtails, I worried. Even though I knew Dale Cooper was up there someplace guarding Vernon in a B-17, I was just *sure* the Germans were going to fly halfway across the United States and bomb us because we were *The County Seat*. I pledged to continue running outside during the daytime when hundreds of big planes rumbled over together, way up high, and make sure they were our planes. That was easy if boys were around because they always called out the numbers: B-29! C-47! P-38!

I think boys liked the war, and wished they could be in it. David Alexander had a big foxhole dug in his grandmother's backyard and played John Wayne so seriously he smoked real cigarettes. This cost him money because when he went to a store to buy them, the merchants knew his parents didn't smoke cheap.

Something else bad about the war: the United States didn't own the whole world anymore. Things like bananas, silk, sugar, and pineapples had to be divided up by giving each family something called ration stamps. Several women once lined up to get enough marshmallows for a party, and every home had an oleo bowl because oleo was white and had to be mixed with orange powder. At least it was fun to say "oleo bowl" and ours had a flower on the side.

Mr. Nauer did what he could to control reckless eating. For example, he refused to sell Albert Roberson two candy bars in one day. "You already had one," he barked. "There's a war going on." But, like the other Vernon merchants, he probably hid bars of soap and other rationed things for his best customers.

There was a *big* shortage of rubber, not even enough for the elastic around the tops of women's underpants. They had to fasten them with buttons and snaps and things. It wasn't uncommon for a lady to be walking down the street and have her underpants fall right down. Most women just stepped out of them and walked on without missing a beat. When it happened to Gladys Eitel on the courthouse walk, she picked them up and tucked them under her arm.

Katie and I made a little money going from door to door selling seeds for victory gardens, even though we didn't know what gardens had to do with winning the war. High school girls knew. They got to skip the first two or three weeks of school those years to go to Dupont and can tomatoes for service men.

The young men had left Vernon. You could tell which houses has sent them because each had a "service banner" hanging in the front window above the ice card. These banners, white satin with gold fringe on the bottom, hung on gold cord fastened to each end of a stick that ran through the top. Dorothy happened to be over at Susie Dibble's the evening before her big brother Paul left. When Dorothy came home she said, "Pauly was sitting on the back steps and said he wanted to be alone to think."

Husbands of our aunts, big brothers of our friends, all the young guys from Shotgun's cardroom left, and throughout the war Vernon got mail and snapshots from them. Harold Bowerly must have sent a snapshot of himself in uniform to every house in town. At family reunions our aunts passed around tablets for everybody to writes notes they could send to their husbands. When women's husbands came home on leave, wives whose husbands weren't home on leave babysat for them, even in the daytime.

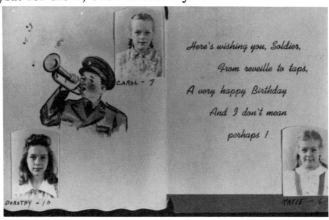

A BIRTHDAY CARD WE SENT GIB HUNT

Finally the war ended and the uncles, the big brothers, and the guys from the cardroom all came home. Harlan Short, who used to come to our house to play cards, did not come home. His body came home.

A big honor board was put up in the courtyard, printed with the names of every person in the county who had served in the war. There were stars beside the names of those who had died. A crowd gathered in the courtyard for a celebration and Mrs. Griessbach sang "The Star Spangled

Banner." Even though our anthem was sung in a German accent, the adults said, "She sang it beautifully."

Vernon never did get bombed, thanks to Dale Cooper up there shouting into his handheld microphone, "First enemy pilot crosses the Muscatatuck's a dead enemy pilot!"

Love Letters

"Convoy!" The cry rang out more frequently after the war ended and our boys were back. As soon as that front jeep was spotted, or somebody heard the rhythmic *zip zip zip* of the troop trucks speeding by, the call was relayed from the middle of town to the river. Girls flocked to the highway. Half-running, half-flying, they acted like Laura Hess's hens when she brought out the cracked corn.

These streaks of khaki set their hearts aflutter as nothing else could. The trucks were khaki, the clothes were khaki. Everything was khaki except the beaming faces of the boys and the blur of their hands throwing out tiny folded-up pieces of paper. I always ran down to the highway, too, to the inside of the curve where the convoy wrapped around us like a warm hug. Taking my position directly behind the bigger girls, I crouched, hands on knees, ready to catch any addresses they missed.

Each time I hoped they wouldn't notice me scratching around in the gravel at their feet, but no sooner was the last truck on the bridge when the big girls would turn to me and demand the one or two addresses clenched in my fists. They pried my fingers open and got them, trying the whole time to sound like mothers. "Soldier boys don't want letters from nine-year-old girls. They want *love* letters."

Then they would run, giggling, into Nellie Stout's house with their treasures. I don't know if they put them all in a pile and divided them evenly like Easter eggs, or if each girl kept her own. "Who cares!" I'd say to myself, and shuffle back up the hill.

One day, however, what I had been praying for happened. A convoy whizzed through town that was so long and so fast those pieces of paper came out in a blizzard. The big girls were much too busy to notice me sticking addresses into my clothing. Because my body was pretty much a straight-up-and-down affair, the clothes my mother made me were full of elastics and I found all kinds of hiding places.

Feeling downright impish by the time the last truck rounded the curve, I clenched my fists anyway and made the big girls pry them open, one finger at a time. When they found nothing, I laughed in their faces. "Ha!" Then I stood and watched them run into Nellie's before I sauntered up the hill, every bit as cool as Grandma's tomcat arriving home at dawn. I went to the outhouse (the only place with a lock on the door) and retrieved the addresses. There were four.

I wrote to these soldiers with full intentions of making every one of them fall in love with me. In spite of what the big girls thought, I knew a lot about romantic love. Because I paid attention to the radio and funny paper ads, I knew poor Milicent should have used her Pepsodent. I knew Pond's lips stayed on and on and on.

And there was all my practicing at Aunt Vonda's dressing table. Many times had I walked to Grandma's house and sat on that padded bench in front of the gigantic round mirror while Vonda was working at the proving ground. I thumbed through her dance books, small pastel things with even tinier pencils attached to them by teeny tiny satin ropes. I tried to imagine what the men looked like who went with the names, real men from real dances, not proms, like the big girls went to. Vonda was a woman.

Occasionally I rearranged the brownish-colored puffs in the pockets of her powder puff doll, a delicate thing made of China, with a wire hoop instead of legs. The skirt was lavender organdy, with lavender bows separating the four pockets at the bottom. Once in awhile I patted just a little of the leftover powder on my face.

I was afraid to put on any of Vonda's Evening in Paris perfume, so I just sniffed it once in awhile. It was in a clear, dark blue bottle about two inches long with a blue string and a tassel fastened to the lid. The bottle wouldn't stand up because it was roundish on the bottom, as if the white-haired scientist who invented this love potion became so excited he left it in the test tube.

Sometimes, while playing Vonda's music box, I held a dance book in one hand and a bottle of Evening in Paris in the other. Waltzing over to the sunlight filtering through Vonda's lace curtains, I would press the vial against the bridge of my nose until all I could see was midnight blue.

Vonda had a gold vanity case that I used for being mysterious. Turned around on the dresser seat, I'd be on a train looking into the vanity case mirror, flirting with a handsome man behind me. We'd be in one of those dining cars with all the little windows. (I'd looked into those windows whenever we got into the Maxwell and drove to North Vernon to watch the trains come and go. Inside every window was a little table with a bouquet of flowers on it, and a tiny lamp that didn't tip over when the train jerked forward.)

The tiniest thing on Vonda's dresser was a red Maybelline brush, all blackened with mascara, but if I'd messed with that my mother would have known for sure. So I held it out a little from my lashes, after using her eyelash curler to "make my eyes whisper romance."

I did tie on a snood, though, if Vonda had left a scarf handy. "Snood" is what the women at the proving ground called the things they bagged up their hair with. Sometimes they used crocheted nets. I thought it was an awful word for something so pretty. *Snood* sounded like a creeper that lurks in dark closets, or a character in the funny papers. Hedy Lamarr looked good in snoods, but they didn't work so well with pigtails.

Before I started my letters to the soldiers, I walked to Grandma's house, made sure she was busy in the kitchen, and went upstairs to Vonda's room for ideas. Then I took my stationery to a place under our apple tree because it seemed the most appropriate place to write the letters. (When I was a *little* girl this was the playhouse where I made mud pies and mixed water with baking powder thrown out from the store.) I told each soldier I wouldn't sit under the apple tree with anybody else but him.

The soldiers' names weren't like the names in Vernon. These names were *long*, and contained a lot of letters from the other end of the alphabet. Each one forced me to pick up my pencil two or three times and look back at the little slip of paper.

Two days after mailing my letters, I began an anxious vigil at the post office. After about four weeks, answers began coming back—three in all—and they were all alike. Reading each one in the courtyard on my way home, I felt my shoulders slump farther with every line. These weren't love letters at all. They *knew*. The soldiers knew I was not a big girl. What had tipped them off? I'd used paper without lines on it. Maybe it was those addresses; they were the biggest addresses I'd ever seen. Maybe they did go uphill a little on my envelopes.

Yet I had applied what I learned from Aunt Vonda's *True Story* and *Modern Romances* magazines, sometimes quoting lines word-for-word. "My heart beats with joyful anticipation when it embraces the thought of our misty eyes meeting for the first time."

But the answers I received weren't romantic at all. They were the kind of letters a fellow would write to a friend...a buddy...a *little sister*. I was so crushed I didn't answer them. I didn't even keep the letters. I threw them away, too naive to know I had held in my hand letters from the most loving kind of guys in the world.

AUNTS

Our mother's three sisters moved in and out of Vernon regularly, which gave us opportunities to be in various sections of town for extended lengths of time. They each lived in the country awhile, too, and those places made for even better visiting.

GRANDMA, ALBERTA, NAOMI, AND VONDA

Naomi

Aunt Naomi, according to our mother, always got to wear the red in the family because she was the one with black hair. Naomi was one of the cooks when our school opened its first lunchroom, in the basement of the old building. Kids could get free lunches there by washing and drying dishes.

Naomi had two sons—Allan, my age, and Denny, who was a year younger than Katie. We played with those boys and fought with them and the fighting was as fun as the playing. While our mothers were in the kitchen talking, we were someplace else having knock-down-drag-outs. I saw the most stars of my life the evening I hit my head on the piano bench and woke up underneath it.

Up by Naomi's house was the best place for catching the ice truck on a hot summer day. We knew when the ice man was coming because women put cards in their windows that were squares divided into four sections by an "X." Each section of the "X" had a number of pounds in it, 25, 50, 75, 100. The housewife sat the card in her window with the number of pounds she wanted at the top.

While the ice man was making deliveries along that street, we'd reach into the back of the truck and get chunks of ice to suck on. It was a pickup truck with a tarp over the bed and a wooden floor all splintery from the tongs. We'd lift our cousin Denny up onto the tailgate because he wanted to get his own ice. One day we didn't get him off in time and the truck went on down the street with Denny on the tailgate and his legs kicking. We all ran along and got him off at the next stop.

The nearest Allan and Denny lived to us was when their daddy, Hank James, was the county sheriff and they lived in the sheriff's end of the courthouse. The jail was in the back part of their house and the jailbirds ate whatever Naomi cooked for her own family. Sometimes we followed her when she took meals to them.

During the time Hank was sheriff, Naomi had a ten-year-old boy as a houseguest and when darkness came, he couldn't be found. The boy was from California, not familiar with Vernon. The deputy sheriff was called down from his North Vernon home to help with the search and soon half the town was combing the riverbanks.

Naomi had been dressed up and ready to leave the house, but after awhile she went back upstairs to put on her old shoes and help with the search. When she leaned over to pick up her shoes, she saw the boy where he had been the whole time, sound asleep under the sheriff's bed.

Hank's dad, Jesse James, had been the Jennings County sheriff, too, and got his name in "Ripley's Believe It or Not" because of it. He later was elected clerk. He was the one who signed our marriage license when Don Layman and I went to the courthouse in the spring of 1956.

Vonda

Although Vonda wasn't the youngest of the Cadby girls, she was the last to get married and leave home. She had dates and we loved that because her boyfriends flirted with us—Vonda would've been just sick if she'd known it—and we got to sit in rumble seats and ride around with them.

Every time Vonda brought a boyfriend to a family dinner, Daddy and the husbands of our other aunts would embarrass her. They would put a stack of catalogs on her boyfriend's chair like they did for the little grandchildren.

In the summertime Vonda wore culottes to her job at the proving ground because she rode around the place all day on a bicycle delivering mail. Once she embarrassed herself when she came in contact with the officer who ran the place. She saw the eagle on his uniform and asked somebody, "Who's the man with the bird on his shoulder?" She sometimes worked a job on the evening shift and almost every night stopped at the Red Duck because the guy she rode with, Ed Bowerly, played the piano there after work. It was a place we kids mentioned only in whispers because we'd heard all kinds of stories about "The Duck," also called, "The Bloody Bucket."

This mysterious place sat beside State Road 7 just north of Dupont in the middle of a semi-circle of tiny "tourist cabins." We knew soldiers drove all the way down to the Red Duck from Camp Atterbury, and that fathers sometimes went in and yanked their daughters right out of the place. We didn't worry about our dad when he played music down there, but we hoped Vonda wasn't near the Red Duck on Saturday nights, when fights got so big they spilled off the dance floor and out into the parking lot. As somebody said, "You pay your way in and fight your way out."

Much to our Grandpa's relief—he once told somebody he couldn't control Vonda—she got married. She married Dave "D. C." Kemper and Grandpa built two more rooms on the end of our house for them to live in. They had their own door and shared our front steps. From time to time Vonda gave me hints about being a wife. One of them was: "When

DAVE KEMPER

your husband gets home in the evening, grab a dish towel and he'll think you've been working. "

Alberta

Alberta was the youngest one in our mother's family. She was only eight years older than my sister Dorothy, and told Dorothy a lot about the facts of life. When Dorothy was a little girl, she got to stay all night at Grandma's and sleep in a big feather bed with Alberta and play "I Spy" until somebody dozed off.

After Alberta married John D. Taylor and they lived in a row house across from the drugstore, Dorothy visited her there. She would sometimes stay all night while John D. was fighting the war in Germany. Dorothy carried in firewood after school because Alberta was expecting a baby. At night she'd roll Alberta's thick hair into a million little pin curls, then they'd eat fudge till they were almost sick.

Alberta loved to sew and cook. After John D. got home from the war he was so proud of her he carried samples of her cakes and biscuits to the neighbors, or whatever farmer he was working for.

Taylors moved to the silver brick house Skyline Bill owned on Brown Street and every day when it was time for John D. to get home from work, Alberta had their little Faye

ALBERTA AND JOHNNY
ON FUNERAL HOME WALL

and Jimmy all dressed up and sitting on the front steps. She fixed herself up, too, and put ribbons in her hair. Their marriage was sure to last.

Clockwise: DAVID LEE KEMPER, JOE EDDIE AND TEDDY SPURLOCK, AND SANDY AND DELORIS KEMPER

JIMMY AND FAYE
TAYLOR WAITING
FOR DADDY

Aunt Betty Comes to Vernon

War, floods, blizzards, tornados, fires...each of them came to Vernon every once in awhile; and every once in awhile Aunt Betty came to Vernon. Our dad's only sibling, she lived in Oklahoma and came back to Vernon in the summertime, but her coming was more than a visit—it was an event.

When she stayed at our house, we brought all our little friends in just to look at her, because she was nothing like the women we knew. To begin with, she had something called "cleavage" and didn't try to hide it. She also smoked cigarettes in cigarette holders and drank and cussed in front of people.

She decorated herself with red nail polish and lots of silver and turquoise Indian jewelry that included big earrings, necklaces, and noisy bracelets.

AUNT BETTY

She always smelled good and wore *real* flowers, in her black hair that was fixed in kind of a bun, and in corsages when it wasn't even a holiday. As soon as a flower started to wilt, she'd hand it to one of us and say, "Here, Honey, give this a decent burial."

Aunt Betty was easy to find in a crowd. We just looked for the biggest hat with the biggest flower on the biggest brim. Or we listened for her laugh. We kids liked to go along when Aunt Betty visited old friends in Vernon because people were so happy to see her. Dorothy said it was like taking them a present. Some of them still laughed about the time she was working in a grocery store in North Vernon when a customer asked for two pounds of bananas. They said Aunt Betty cut one banana in two to get the correct weight.

When she came back to Vernon to visit, she sat outside our house some evenings and we could easily spy on her and her company, usually men and never just one. We got such a kick out of watching the men because they suddenly became different from the way we knew them. Their faces would get red, and they giggled like little boys, or laughed out loud a lot, at things she said that weren't even funny. But most of the things she said *were* funny.

Dorothy saw this a lot when she graduated from high school and went to nurses training in Tulsa, where Aunt Betty lived. She said whether Aunt Betty was on a bus, a train, or a plane, a crowd would be gathered around her, men and women. At the end of the trip there would be a great flurry of address exchanges.

While we were sure the men liked Aunt Betty, we didn't know what the women thought of her because as soon as we went into the kitchen, where they would be sitting at the table and leaning against the cupboards, they would quit talking. Aunt Betty didn't seemed concerned about the women talking, but she often thanked God because *things* couldn't talk..."Thank God that school building can't talk...If that state park could talk...Thank Goodness those walls can't talk."

She was a former nurse, married to a doctor who seldom came to Vernon with her. On one of his trips we got him to look at our neighbor, Vail Hartwell, because we were worried about her heart. A few times Aunt Betty brought her kids and rented one of the Whitcomb apartments for the entire summer. Once she brought a maid, too.

She and our dad were orphans raised by their mother's adopted parents, the Kimpels. Part of the time Aunt Betty said their mother had been left on the Kimpel's Indianapolis doorstep by gypsies. Other times she said their mother was the illegitimate daughter of a bachelor professor at Hanover College named Richard Souter. Her accounts of our family history weren't too reliable. She said our grandfather had died in an air force plane crash during World War I, but we heard less glamorous accounts from other people.

She said all the Spurlocks left England on the same date…in the middle of the night.

At least we had newspaper clippings to tell us the truth about our great-grandfather Kimpel, a red-headed giant who had been an Indianapolis policeman twenty-seven years before he retired to Jennings County. He left the force known as the only man among over 400 to be wearing a beard and mustache, in spite of the unwritten rule against them.

As for Aunt Betty, things just seemed to happen around her. She was taking a nap at our house once when Riley Bowerly's horses got tired waiting for him at a field he worked down beyond Engle's bridge. They ran all the way through town pulling that empty wagon. When they crossed the south curve and hit the gravel between the highway and Shotgun's gas pumps, they made an awful racket. Aunt Betty sat straight up in bed, then walked around the house at least ten minutes holding her cigarette up, cussing those horses, and looking for an ashtray.

Some of the things Aunt Betty said…well, I *knew* they weren't true, but I thought about them late at night. For example, one afternoon when the locomotive engine was sitting on the trestle blowing off steam she said, "Some day that engine's going to blow up and nuts and bolts will rain on Vernon for two hours." Then she leaned her head back, closed her eyes, took a puff on her cigarette holder, and blew the smoke like she wasn't a bit afraid.

Here's the scariest one: "Some day that highway's going to straighten itself out and wipe half of Vernon off the map." I often wondered, lying in bed on my way to sleep, what kind of sound that would make. Would it be a sudden "Wham!" like a screen door with a tight spring? Or would we have a warning, maybe a slow, creaking sound? Would it go "Boing!"? Would it make a grinding noise? Then I knew what the sound would be. It would be "Plooooog!"

Every Vernon kid knew every other Vernon kid, but each of us had those few we spent more time with. My three closest friends were Joyce Whitcomb, Cynthia Crist, and Charlona Ochs. We got to know each other's families very well, too. For some reason, we were all afraid of each other's dads and aimed to avoid them, making it a point to be gone before they got home.

None of my closest friends lived in large families. They could let their mothers know when they were mad by not speaking, or by pouting.

SHIRLEY STAGGS, CHARLONA OCHS, CYNTHIA CRIST, JOYCE WHITCOMB, TOOTSIE FRY, AND JOAN JOHNSON

If you did that in a family like mine, nobody noticed.

Charlona

Charlona Ochs lived in a house built on the basement where her grandpa's home had sat, on a little hill surrounded by a big yard. The front walk was made of bricks from the first house and curved its way down to the cemetery road. I walked to school with Charlona whenever I had spent the night next door with my Aunt Vonda. Every morning while I stood outside Charlona's house, doves would be cooing in the trees that edged the school yard across the road.

Charlona was Katie's age and the three of us played together a lot, but she spent more time with me alone as we got older because we both twirled batons. She was very neat

SANDRA LAYMAN, CHARLONA OCHS,
J.W. COOMBS, AND DONNIE LAYMAN

and sometimes took two or three showers a day in the summer.

Her older brother, Bert, and two other high school boys sang and played instruments at convocations. They even had a weekly show on the Seymour radio station. A kind of fan club among the North Vernon girls chased after Bert. I was with Charlona once when they tried to get her to steal things out of his dresser drawers for them. She refused to do it. Bert scared everybody by getting polio in high school, but he recovered.

Hellen Ochs was a pretty and petite lady with a bubbly personality who fixed herself up more than most Vernon women. She did clever things like send Charlona's written excuses to school on paper doilies, or invite friends for a ham supper, then serve fried bologna. She was probably the one who got the idea of naming Charlona after her daddy Charles and her grandma Lona Wildey.

RAY REYNOLDS, HELEN WALT, BENNY BARBER, AND
GLENN SLONE

206

For a long time I thought Charlona's grandpa Ochs was Mark Twain. Sitting on his high front porch catty-cornered from Madge Jordan's house, he looked just like the picture of Mark Twain on our Authors cards. His

MIKE ROGERS, JUDY ALEXANDER, SUSIE ROGERS, AND ELAINE ROSEBERRY

hair was white and he wore the same kind of mustache. Even if he wasn't Mark Twain, he must have been important; he *owned* Bluebell Island.

Because of Charlona I got to go to Louisville, more than once, during the years Hellen had some kind of a part-time decorator job in a downtown department store. She went to Madison sometimes and dropped us girls off at the pool.

On one of those swimming trips I saw something in the dressing room that really disgusted me. Big girls were parading around without any clothes on instead of staying behind the curtains where they belonged. It was the first time I had ever seen what women were supposed to look like naked. I hardly swam at all that day; I just sat on the edge of the pool and shivered, trying to decide if I really wanted a body like that when I grew up.

Charlona's family moved away just before her senior year, so she didn't get to continue the Ochs tradition of graduating from Vernon High School.

Cynthia

Cynthia was like an only child because she had been born when the other Crist kids were already married and gone. Dorothy once embarrassed our mother by asking Mrs.

Crist if she was Cynthia's grandma. With long, blond curls and dark brown eyes, Cynthia was the prettiest among us Vernon girls. The boys noticed her at an early age, long before they noticed the rest of us.

She made us Spurlocks nervous when she got on her maroon bicycle to go home. She'd zoom down the hill and across the highway without looking either way. When she eventually got hit by a green pickup truck that came whizzing around the curve, I saw her body fly straight up into the air, then land on the pavement. Grandpa went out and carried her to the back of the store and laid her on the bed. Her mother got the word and came down from the other side of town on foot, all huffing and red-faced. But Cynthia was okay; she didn't have to go to a hospital or anything.

Cynthia and I got to be alone in her house a lot. Her dad worked at Indianapolis all week and was home only on weekends. Her mother, known as one of the best cooks in Jennings, worked evenings, usually in some restaurant or the country club. Sometimes when her mother had to work late, I stayed all night at Cynthia's.

One of the best things at their house was a tall, windup Victrola. We usually played Frank Sinatra records and danced together, taking turns having to be the man. When we played their older, brown records, we put spools on the spindle for weight because they wanted to curl up.

I very seldom saw Cynthia's dad's face. To me, Mr. Crist was two hands holding an open newspaper with puffs of cigar smoke coming up from behind it every so often. From behind that newspaper he answered any conversation with grunts or little growling noises. I saw the back of his head a lot because I sometimes went riding with Cynthia on Sunday afternoons. They were quiet rides. Being in Mr. Crist's car was not like being in a Maxwell full of Spurlocks. And Mr. Crist's car went someplace besides Cherry Park. We often went to Grayford, even down through Kentucky.

We read Burma Shave signs along the way, and barns that told us to "See Rock City" and "Chew Mail Pouch."

Cynthia's mother was an important person in our church. She was a good singer—she looked and sounded like an opera singer—and you could hear her hit those high notes above everybody else. She had Cynthia taking piano lessons at an early age and playing the piano at church when she was in junior high school. She often talked to Cynthia and me about manners, Christianity, and other important things in life.

Mrs. Crist was generous with her cooking, but other Vernon women complained because she wouldn't give out her recipes. She got another kind of complaint one Sunday during her turn to entertain the preacher and his wife, who came up from the Louisville seminary on weekends. When the wife saw Cynthia's mother heap up a big plate of food and put a cover on it, she asked who it was for. "Ben Henry," Mrs. Crist said, "that man across the street sitting on his porch."

DONNIE ENGLE AND CECIL ARNEY

The lady craned her neck and looked out the window. "But he's *culud*!" she exclaimed in her sweet, southern accent. Mrs. Crist went right ahead and sent the food over to Ben anyway. That was a lesson we'd never forget.

Toward the end of high school, Cynthia was planning her marriage to a North Vernon boy named Jimmy O'Mara and was looking at furniture. They had been dating for quite some time. "But when I get married, it won't be because I *have* to," Cynthia always said. "I won't give Maggie Abbett the pleasure." And she didn't.

Joyce

Both sides of Joyce's family went way back in Vernon history. Her mother, Lois, had been childless until Joyce was born in her 40th year. Lois Whitcomb played solitaire a lot because Joyce's dad was often busy in the evenings, especially after he opened the Skate-Bowl between Vernon and North Vernon in 1949. He'd take a whole carload of Vernon kids up there to skate.

When he was home, Joyce and I tiptoed around because he usually was stretched out on the couch with his forearm across his head—sinus trouble or something. He often made head-clearing noises. During the war he was a warden, just like my dad, only he had a huge map fastened over his davenport so he could keep track of the war all over the world, not just in Vernon.

Joyce's and Cynthia's mothers both belonged to the Clionian Society, a Vernon club believed to be the oldest women's club in Indiana. Joyce's dad was a director of the Jennings Building and Loan, so if that group met the same night as the Clionian Club, she had to go with her dad. In the winter she sat with the men around the pot-bellied stove in Wenzel's Hardware. That was embarrassing for her because she had once gone in there for some tenpenny nails and asked for "ten cent nails."

Joyce had interesting things at her house. She had a little hat pin cushion her neighbor Granny Jones had crocheted for her, and Joyce's dad had made her bunk doll beds with pencils for spindles. Whitcombs had one of the first television sets in Vernon and I liked to watch "I Love Lucy" on their living room carpet instead of in the crowded filling station.

I soon got to know Joyce's neighborhood very well. The beer joint was across the street from Joyce and sometimes kept her awake on Saturday nights. When walking to each other's houses, we crossed the highway so as not to pass directly in front of it. At least the men who left the place usually did it on foot.

GRANNY JONES ACROSS THE STREET FROM MAGGIE ABBETT'S HOUSE

One man who lived beyond Engle's bridge would ask Vernon boys to walk him to the culvert at night. "I want you to show me which hole to go through," he'd say. I guess he was too drunk to know the culvert had only one hole.

Sandefur's house was next door to Joyce. They were the first family in town to have those bubble lights on their Christmas tree. Whenever they cleaned out their flue, Granny

DADDY AND BOB LUNSFORD
AT OUR HOUSE

Jones would come over and get some soot for making little cakes. Granny Jones was from Switzerland and her husband had been Welsh, so it must have been a recipe from one of those countries. Vernon kids didn't eat any.

Sandefurs seemed to deliver all the papers and magazines in town and had a wagon with more miles on it than anybody's. Their parents sent them and their wagon to the mill for coal, to the store for groceries, and to the homes of Old Dutch Cleanser women to take food. After they'd unloaded the food, they used the wagon to move kindling and wood from these women's sheds to their stoves.

Their dad helped our Girl Scout troop—Vernon had one for awhile but no uniforms or anything like that. When we got ready to make first aid kits out of those flattish tobacco cans with hinged lids, Rosanna Sandefur took them home and her daddy chrome plated them at Shackleford's in North Vernon, where he worked. Then we painted a big red cross on each one with fingernail polish and filled them with first aid supplies.

Three corners of the block Joyce lived on were occupied by Whitcombs. Joyce's uncle, Robert "Buck" Whitcomb, taught school at North Vernon. David Alexander rode with him because he wanted to finish school there after moving to Vernon. David said Buck Whitcomb was the slowest driver in the world. "He's what started the expression 'pass the buck,'" David said.

NANCY STAGMAN, DOROTHY ROBERSON, AND MARCELLA
GRANT WITH STAFFORD PROPERTY IN BACKGROUND

Joyce's grandpa, Shep Whitcomb, was known by every kid in school even though he was no longer superintendent. He was blind because of diabetes, and had an artificial leg we could examine anytime we wanted to. Those things didn't keep him from singing at our commencements. He lived in the big brick house across the street from the school. It was the old seminary building and still had blackboards on the backs of the doors.

Mr. Whitcomb came over to our school sometimes to visit. All he had to do was stand at the end of the sidewalk and before long kids would be fighting over who got to help him. Once in the building—the gym building because it had fewer steps—he told stories to large groups, or sat at a low table in a little room and let five or six children at a time read to him or discuss things. Some kids went to his house for special tutoring.

Shep Whitcomb had something called "talking books" at his house, records of people reading. Roberson's older brother, Albert, would walk up to Whitcomb's and listen to the talking books with him. Albert had only one tenth of his vision because of catching the measles at age nine.

Grandma Whitcomb wrapped her hair around one of those separate hair pieces women called "rats." They made these rats by raking their own hairs out of their brushes and forming them into rolls. When Mrs. Whitcomb wasn't wearing her rat, she kept it in a special dish on her dresser.

It was something like what Aunt Betty wore only Aunt Betty had hers made at a beauty shop and called it by some French name.

Joyce's cousin Andy Anderson was visiting their grandma and grandpa in 1948 when the back part of the big house caught fire. "Andy!" Grandma Whitcomb said, "run in and get my rat off the dresser!" Joyce and I didn't know if the rat was her grandma's most valuable possession, or if she just didn't want the firemen to see it.

MARY LOU PATTERSON, *front*, AND FRIENDS ON THE OLD STAR SHE BOUGHT FROM MARK RIESER. *L. to R.*, RUTH CASTER, MARGIE FRY, JOAN ST. JOHN, DONNA HEATON, DOROTHY ASH, AND MARJORIE STEWART

LAMPLIGHTER DAYS

We were glad Vernon was already modern...until the radio played "The Old Lamplighter," then we wished Vernon still had streetlights with fire in them. Simpson's mother, Florence, remembered when Vernon *did* have a man who went around lighting the streetlamps, but was unable to remember his name. She said everyone called the man "Lexie the lamplighter."

He pushed a cart that was about a yard square and full of cans of coal oil with wicks sticking out of the tops. She said he would open the glass door on a streetlamp in the evening, take out the empty can from the night before, and replace it with a lighted can, one that contained just enough oil to light up the corner until decent folks went to bed.

Lucille Bolser could talk about "the night they turned the lights on in Vernon." It was in 1916, she said. Lena Willman was elected the queen who got to throw the switch.

Lots of older people remembered back when Vernon's electricity came from a generator George Ale ran near the firehouse. He had wired the town and ran the generator during the day. He left it on late when something was going on in Vernon, and fired it up early on Monday and Tuesday mornings so Vernon women could wash and iron. That didn't sound so fun. It made us realize we wanted our electricity, but on snowy winter evenings around Christmas, we wanted a lamplighter, too.

Water piped from North Vernon came to Vernon just before we were born. The only sign of the old system was the standpipe on the ridge, sitting atop a stone foundation beside the Presbyterian Church. Boys who climbed the ladder to the top and slid down the guy wires said it was empty, except for rain water and old dead birds.

When our mother was a girl, there was a chug-chug generating station down by Engle's bridge that sent water

from the Muscatatuck up to the standpipe so it could run back down to Vernon's houses. She said there was a round trough sitting on that main line where it passed in front of the courthouse.

This trough, for horses to drink from, was filled through a valve in the line. Our mother said she liked to look into this trough on her way to the post office because there were always little fish swimming around in it. Hmm.

WHEN THE STANDPIPE WAS NEW

HORSE TROUGH IN FRONT OF COURTHOUSE

Left: SEMINARY BUILDING WITH LAMP AT CORNER

1932 TORNADO; BUILDINGS THAT WERE REPLACED BY SHAW APTS.

1932 TORNADO; THE BUILDINGS BETWEEN THE FLOUR MILL AND
SKYLINE BILL'S HOTEL WERE REMOVED.

MEALTIME IN VERNON

Some outsiders got confused about meals in Vernon, yet it was all very simple: The midday meal was called *dinner*, unless you ate it at school or work. Then it was called *lunch*.

Dads carried their lunches to work in black things called *dinner buckets* that looked like little coffins with handles on them. The evening meal was called *supper*, unless

DINNER AT CADBY'S - *Clockwise*: DENNY JAMES (*back to camera*), HANK JAMES, DADDY, JOHN TAYLOR, ME, GRANDMA, UNCLE LLOYD, DOROTHY, ALLAN, AND KATIE, *sticking out tongue*

you ate it out, then you said, "We went out for dinner," but Vernon people hardly ever did that.

Supper at our house was like a circus. Daddy would say funny things, then anybody who laughed too long had to go into the bedroom and get it out of the system. Not liking emotional displays was one thing, but we didn't understand what was so wrong with laughter at the table.

DINNER AT LAYMAN'S - *Clockwise*: SANDRA'S CHAIR, GRANDPA GEORGE LAYMAN, GRANDMA ROSA, HAROLD, D'ETTE, DON, AND ME

Usually, he just pointed toward the door to the bedroom and the emotional person left the room. He once suggested Dorothy was getting fat and she jumped to her feet and slammed a slice

JAKE SWARTHOUT EATING WITH
BOGGSES - *L. to R.*: BERNADINE,
BUTCH, KAREN, RANDY, AND SARAH

of bread into a bowl of soup so hard it splashed all over him. She was afraid he would get mad, but we could tell he was trying to keep from laughing.

Whenever we pointed to what we wanted passed instead of asking for it, Daddy would call us by the name of a certain man in Vernon who was said to do that. This was Vernon shorthand; just the mention of a name could get a message across. If we got up from the table and moved a curtain to look out the window, he would have called us by another Vernon name.

When I started dating Don Layman I ate at his house a lot. They had a dining room, and meals there were a little more dignified than they were at our house. And it was Don who took me out to a restaurant for my first steak dinner. I started pulling the meat apart with my knife and fork as soon as I got my meal. "*What* are you doing?" he asked with a bewildered look on his face.

"Looking for shot," I answered, as if he should know.

o━o━o━o━o━o━o━o

Another Little-Known Fact about Vernon

William Shaw, John Dillinger's driver and partner in crime, stayed in Vernon one summer with his aunt when he was a boy in the 1920s. His career with Dillinger ended with his arrest in 1933.

220

CELEBRITIES

The more important people were, the less we saw them. I never saw Powell Crosley, Jr., who owned 2,000 acres just south of Vernon where fourteen people worked. This was his private hunting place with a timber lodge, lake, stables, and swimming pool. He also had a landing strip so he could fly in from Cincinnati, where he was a big shot. Local people called his estate "the place." No gates were on it, so you could drive right through and then tell your friends, "We drove through the place Sunday."

Crosley, as we called him, made appliances, including his *Shelv-a-door*, the first refrigerator with shelves in the door, and he made tiny cars named after himself. He remembered people who didn't have electricity yet and produced many things especially for them, like his "icy ball" refrigerators. He owned the WLW radio station in Cincinnati and even owned the Reds, who often visited his lodge.

Being a good dancer, he rented local places and threw dances for his Cincinnati friends and for local people. Our daddy played his banjo for these dances sometimes. Once he didn't get home until daylight and our mother was worried because she knew the dances usually ended at midnight. This one was held over a store at North Vernon but Daddy couldn't call her because we didn't have a phone yet.

When he got home, he said Crosley had the band go out to his lodge and play the rest of the night.

CROSLEY'S PLACE

Mr. Crosley's family and friends would come to his retreat. Cincinnati ladies dressed in their riding clothes, including those pants that flared out at the hips, were quite a contrast to the farmers who stood by the fences and watched them go by on the bridle paths.

While still a young man, Mr. Crosley had worked as a day laborer on the construction of the Indianapolis 500 race track. "A down-to-earth kind of guy," is what his local employees called him. "You wouldn't know he had money," one of them said.

He gave Crosley radios to his Jennings County neighbors for Christmas and all his workers were invited to his Cincinnati home for the holidays. He once insisted that an employee's parents celebrate their golden wedding anniversary there. The first time he took his workers to a Reds game he planned to have them all for dinner at his house. His farm boss, Kenneth Deputy, talked him into having it in a restaurant instead of his home. "Some of my boys are pretty rough," Mr. Deputy had said.

HENRY HULSE SELLING CROSLEY RADIOS

A celebrity who spent summers in Vernon was Albert Edward Wiggam, a graduate of Vernon High School. He lived in New York City and wrote books, also a newspaper column called, "Let's Explore Your Mind." We read it in our Sunday *Star*. The sales of one book had increased after William Jennings Bryan criticized it in the Scopes trial.

Dr. Wiggam, who was called "Ed" on Front Street, was tall and had bad eyes. He said he used his wife's eyes. If you came down the alley and their windows were open, you could hear her reading to him, or typing. She was a city person who wore lots of jewelry and seldom came outside when they were in Vernon, but she was nice. Nancy Stagman and Carol Kingen worked for her sometimes. She'd send them to pick violets down toward the river, telling them to make all the stems the same length. She gave Carol a cute bench.

Her husband did a lot of writing in Vernon, which one reviewer called "a quaint little old-world town." His Vernon house, next to Mrs. Reese, looked like it could have been designed by Mark Twain—white frame with green shutters and a white picket fence. Neighbor children got to sit on his porch and listen to him tell stories

ALBERT E. WIGGAM

while his wife served them lemonade. Caroling kids who were lucky enough to be invited into their house when they were here for Christmas said they had a baby grand piano.

Dr. Wiggam once gave dimes to Carol and Benny Ray Johnson, but Carol threw hers away in some weeds because her mother had told her never to take money from strangers.

Things to Do with an Outdated Sears Catalog

Fold the heavy, colored pages into cootie catchers, snappers, airplanes, or pleated fans, or cut them into strips and make round or zigzag chains. Cut out curtained windows and rooms of furniture and lay out houses on the floor. Cut out people for the houses. Cut slits just beneath the pillows in the bed pictures and stick the people's heads through so it will look like they're in bed. Try to make paper dolls by matching people from the catalog with clothes from the catalog. Cut the heads off the people and put them on each other's bodies. (That is *really* funny.)

If a war is going on and the catalog has to go directly to the outhouse for use as toilet paper, hurry and tear out all those soft, pastel-colored index pages and hide them for yourself. It's worth it, even if your sisters do curl their lips and call you "Princess Elizabeth."

MISSING THE CURVES

Vehicles were always running off the curves in Vernon, especially the north curve, which seemed to be banked the wrong way. There were some mean wrecks up there.

One time a semi wheel chased Skinny Walt all the way home.

NORTH CURVE WRECK

Charlie Elliott had a little shed propped up there in that neighborhood and he'd collect for damages every time somebody ran over it. Then he'd prop it back up in just the right spot for the next sucker. He said that shed paid his house off.

Granny Jones was sitting in her favorite window doing handiwork when somebody overshot the middle curve and plowed right into that window. It was some crazy man driving a motor scooter. He was *standing on the seat of the thing*. The only injury Granny Jones suffered was a goose egg from a flower pot that fell on her head.

MIDDLE CURVE WRECK

Somebody behind the wheel of a Model A Ford came around our curve too fast one Saturday night—or early Sunday morning—on his way home from the Red Duck. He drove into the courtyard, almost to the treasurer's office, taking out a small maple tree on the way.

SOUTH CURVE WRECK; WWII HONOR ROLL AT LEFT

A few years later a girl came around there and made a left turn in front of an oncoming vehicle, which of course hit her. "I had my left turn signal on," she told the deputy.

"That's right, officer," said her father, "she had her left turn signal on."

One morning we thought we were seeing the results of a bad accident. We looked out the stairway window and discovered a bicycle high on top of the Pure Oil sign across the highway. Then we remembered...it was Halloween.

IF A 1940s CAR HIT A BUILDING, IT WASN'T THE CAR THAT SUFFERED

TED BENNETT'S BASKETBALL STORIES

Our daddy's friend, Ted Bennett, was a basketball nut. Through him we learned about the early basketball days at Vernon High School. He said they began in 1911 when sawdust was scattered on the ground and a single goal post put up in front of the academy building. The arena was almost unlimited because it was possible for the ball to roll all the way to the river.

A few years later Prof Jackson put together the first official Vernon Blue Devils team, a group of boys with no uniforms, no showers, and sometimes no substitutes. A girls' team, the Devilettes, was formed that same year, 1914, even though the people of Vernon were "against" girls' basketball. The girls not only played by boys' rules, they played the boys. They would soon be playing before every boys' home game.

No practice was allowed during school hours for the Vernon Blue Devils. The boys stayed after school two days a week, then walked as many as three miles to their homes. Prof did not attend the practices. In 1915, Ted said, the boys went down and played the employees of Craigmont, a mental institution at North Madison. Because the games usually were held outdoors—"Scipio had the best outdoor court in the county,"—the season ended at Thanksgiving.

Some of Vernon's home games were held in Hengstler Hall, upstairs over Mr. Nauer's earlier drugstore. The ceiling was low up there and the size of the playing court was determined by the number of people who came and stood around the walls to watch. A freewill offering was taken to cover expenses.

Ted made getting to the "away" games sound as fun as the games themselves. The southern river towns were their favorite foes, he said, because they rode to Madison on the train, then went by boat to Vevay, or Rising Sun, or other towns on the Ohio. One night in 1918 they met with a rough Ohio River on their return trip and got back to school the next morning just in time for their first class.

A week-long tournament was held every year at Columbus, in the county northwest of us. Ted said the tourney was open to "all the teams in this part of the state who could get there." Some years the Vernon boys were lucky to be able to stay with former Vernonites who had moved to Columbus.

Butlerville, one of Vernon's local opponents in Ted's day, had two guys who would go together to shoot a basket. The smaller one would hop onto the shoulders of the tall one and put the ball in the hoop. There was nothing in the rule book against this, so they did it many times. This stunt was how Butlerville beat Vernon 16 to 15 with a last-minute shot in the Seymour sectional in 1923. After a protest to the commissioner, the shot was outlawed in the rule book.

Ted said the Vernon boys were always lost when they played in a gym, and so were the Vernon fans, it seems. He said our daddy, being a friend of his, was allowed to ride with the team to a game at Paris Crossing, where the gym was illuminated by a gasoline generator. Daddy, being a country boy used to lamps and lanterns, stuck his finger in an empty socket and all the lights went dim while he was knocked out of his chair. He wasn't hurt though...and the game continued.

"The No Gyms" is what the Vernon boys were called, but they did the best they could, sometimes by renting the gym at North Vernon High School for practice. Thank goodness I didn't have to suffer any of that humiliation because by the time I started school, we had a brand-new gym of our own. A home game brought out all the people in Vernon and cars lined the hill streets from top to bottom. All four rows of our bleachers would be filled and chairs set up on the stage.

Some rivalries that had developed among Jennings County's nine high schools in those early years were still going strong when we hit high school in the 1950s, but only four high schools were still in existence then: Vernon, Paris Crossing, Hayden, and the much larger North Vernon.

Lucky for us, North Vernon didn't participate in the annual county

PROF JACKSON AND HIS 'NO GYMS' - *Front*: ROGER WHITCOMB, TED BENNETT, AND JACK RILEY. *Back*: JESS WHITCOMB, LEE ROGERS, DUDLEY CHILDS, WALTER CARSON, WILLIAM SHUCK, AND BROOKS RILEY

tourney, so the rest of us always had a shot at bringing home the plaster of paris trophy called "Leo the Lion." Vernon never won a sectional, but no sectional crown could have compared with being the best county school in Jennings.

<hr />

Another Little-Known Fact about Vernon

One summer in the 1940s, all the kittens born in Vernon were spastic. They had small fits and jerked their heads around all the time. "Too much interbreeding," said the Cartwright grandma, "need some fresh tomcats." Fresh tomcats were brought in from the country and the problem was solved.

The human babies born in Vernon that summer were okay.

Yet Another Little-Known Fact, Or at Least a Legend, about Vernon

Two Vernon men, a big man and a small man, ordered their suits from Sears & Roebuck at the same time and on credit. The big man ordered a suit to fit the small man, and the small man ordered a suit to fit the big man. As soon as the suits arrived, they traded them but never sent in their money.

When the bill collector came to the big man's house, the big man looked at the paper and said, "Do I look like I could wear a suit that size?" The small man did the same thing, and the two men never paid for their suits.

BOB SHAW'S COURTHOUSE MADE OF MATCHSTICKS

THE CHERRY PARK CAMPERS

The Cherry Park campers were nothing more than Shotgun's cardroom gang moved out into the country. They had this spot called Spaulding Hole, two miles east of Vernon on the south fork of the Muscatatuck, where a beautiful rock wall curved around and reflected in the water. A high limb on a huge sycamore that leaned out over the swimming hole had a rope tied to it for swinging out and letting go.

SPAULDING HOLE

Every August the men packed all their camping gear and went out there for a week to fish, hunt, play cards, drink spring water (and other things), sit around in their underwear, not shave, and let go. At first, having no shelter over their beds of leaves and straw, they used a funeral tent given to them by Jordans. Eventually they bought army cots and two tents.

Our daddy was one of the men who started this. Spaulding Hole was down a lane on the farm where he grew up and he took us out there a lot. If the men were camping, he had to announce that he was bringing girls in. The rest of the year nobody was there and he was just checking the place, and his drop lines.

At the Cherry Park camp, men who didn't cook at home, cooked, if you want to call dumping two boxes of rolled oats into a pot that boiled over and put out the fire *cooking*. It was a place where the jokes they played on each other were so bad we couldn't even hear about them. One booby trap that backfired was a two-foot hole in the path they'd filled with water and cow manure and covered with grass. Our mother and Fry's mother, Oral, were the ones who stepped in it, and they were wearing white shoes.

The campers took their sons out there practically as soon as they were born. The boys visited during the day until they were old enough to stay all night. One day when Gib Hunt got thirsty he asked Joe Skinner's son, Roger, to "Open me up a can of something." Roger went into the kitchen tent, turned the can opener around, and brought Gib out a can of peaches. Gib drank those peaches right down, like a college boy drinking goldfish.

GIB HUNT DRINKING PEACHES WHILE DADDY AND JOE
SKINNER LOOK ON IN DISBELIEF

HOLIDAYS

The least fun holiday in Vernon was New Year's Eve. After a long struggle to stay awake until midnight, our only reward was hearing a combination of car horns, gun blasts, and church bells…and Daddy's beagles howling at the church bells.

Easter meant a big egg hunt in the church yard on Saturday, which was good for us Spurlocks because we could go back up there after everybody left and find a few more eggs. Easter Sunday was the Sunday everybody dressed up the most and people would come to church who hadn't been there all year. They were usually dressed better than anybody.

EASTER – *L. to R.*: CHARLENE DUDLEY, KATIE, SUSIE DIBBLE, MARY LOU, DOROTHY, ME, AND RAMONA DUDLEY

May Day was a holiday my friend Joyce and I celebrated together. About the middle of April we started cutting and pasting two dozen little construction-paper baskets, making handles on them big enough to hang on doorknobs. To fill these baskets we had to get up very early on May Day morning and pick enough violets and other wild flowers. (We couldn't pick them the day before, or they would have wilted.) Then we went around to the houses of special Vernon women, usually older women, and hung the baskets on their front doors.

Halloween was good. It was the only time we got into certain houses. From behind our false faces we gave them a good looking over while the people who lived there tried to guess who we were. When the Wolfinger girls went trick-or-treating, their daddy put a white sheet over himself, got on his big white stallion, and followed them along Vernon's streets. Mary Jane and Bobby Jean probably got extra candy because the housewives were busy looking at their daddy.

Knowing what kind of treat would be waiting at each house, everybody made beelines to VanGorden's and Dick and Betty Willman's. Mrs. VanGorden gave out delicious popcorn balls, each one wrapped in waxed paper. Dick gave us nickels, enough to buy a bottle of pop, or a piece of Mrs. Welker's pie. Dick Willman loved kids, maybe because he had been mischievous as a boy, over and above the usual boy test of stealing a watermelon out of Mr. Griessbach's garden. He and Wilford Day even set a gas well on fire down towards the Commons.

Thanksgiving meant an aunts-uncles-cousins dinner at Grandma's, and the main question: Will I finally be old enough this year to sit in the dining room with the big people, or will they make me sit in the kitchen again with the little brats?

In December we started seeing signs of Christmas coming. Each Spurlock kid looked through the Sears' Christmas book and picked out two things we would like to have Santa Claus bring us, or even more if the total was not over five dollars. Then came the time to start practicing the Christmas program at church, held every year on Christmas Eve because there was no place else in the world to be on that special night but in the church.

After we had said our pieces or acted in a play, each of us sat on Santa's lap and told him what we wanted for

Christmas. Then he gave us a sack containing an orange, peanuts, and candy, which we had helped count out on a long table in Grandpa's store.

Our hearts as well as our feet would be pounding when we ran down the hill after the program. We'd said our pieces or played a part in the nativity scene, Santa Claus was going to put presents under our cedar Christmas tree that night, and the snow starting to fall looked like diamond dust.

ROSSES' DAIRY BAR AT CHRISTMAS;
DOROTHY ROBERSON BEHIND COUNTER

Another Little-Known Fact about Vernon

Ben Johnson, who played musical instruments and sang in public with his brothers, heard a knock at his front door one winter night. He opened the door to find his neighbor, Paul Hunt, standing there in pajamas. "Bring that guitar out here," Paul said, while Ben just stood blinking his eyes. "You didn't know I could play, did you?" Paul said with a laugh.

"Paul, it's 1:30 in the morning," Ben said. "It's cold, and you're barefooted!" Paul wouldn't back down, so Ben went in and got his guitar and Paul Hunt sat there on Johnson's front porch picking out "The Spanish Fandango" while tapping his chubby, bare foot on the cold concrete. After he'd finished the song, he went back home and the Johnsons went back to bed.

Just another night in Vernon.

BOB SHAW'S FLOUR MILL MADE OF MATCHSTICKS

SNOW

I liked snow and felt sorry for kids who didn't have our winter wonderlands. Sometimes on hot August days I'd walk down to the store, take a box of cornstarch off the shelf, close my eyes, and squeeze the box at regular intervals. That's what sound-effect men on the radio did when a person was supposed to be walking in snow. When I did it, I pictured snow up by the church, at night, under the streetlight, where the whole earth sparkled like a sugar cookie.

In winter, when the snow was real, I felt sorry for those certain girls always singled out by the town bullies to get their faces washed. I also felt sorry for kids who lived in towns without hills. Vernon's best hill was Madge Jordan's. Madge Jordan even brought out hot chocolate sometimes, but Madge Jordan didn't drive. About every hill had one man who drove and he would bring out a bucket of cinders from his coal stove and lay a strip across the road for traction. Most of the time, though, one hill was left alone for us to use.

We Spurlocks usually slid on our own hill, day and night and at least long enough to make it worthwhile to put on all those leggin's, snowsuits, hats, mittens, and galoshes.

BETTY JO SCUDDER AND MARY GRINSTEAD

When we were done for the day, we'd slide right up to our door. A wooden clothes rack waited behind the stove for us, and the front room smelled like hot, wet wool the rest of the night. I never understood why, if we got a cold, it was always caused by sledding, never by carrying in wood and coal for the stove, which was one of the times we accused our parents of having us just for slaves.

The best kinds of snows were those deep enough to close school, like the blizzard of '50, which began on a Saturday night at the end of November. Twelve inches of snow fell and blew into high drifts. Sunday morning everybody in Vernon, even the old people, said the same thing: "I've never seen snow this deep." Tanks were brought out of the armory at North Vernon to clean off the highways, but for the most part, everything in Jennings County stopped but the rumors.

One which turned out to be true was that Cecil Hartwell, who worked nights in the railroad yards at North Vernon, had his leg run over by a train. His wife later said the cold snow probably saved his life, but it made the rescue awfully slow.

A big north-south bus that usually passed through Vernon looked funny parked in front of Welker's Lunch. The cooks recruited anybody within walking distance to help wait on them. Dorothy went down to help and found the tiny little place packed. She said there were some Negro people in back of the bus who wouldn't come in and eat, even though Vernon people tried to get them to.

The stories we heard about cars being stranded along the south highways because of blizzards were always true. Out on State Road 3, Florence Simpson once cooked breakfast for seventeen strangers. Her electricity was out, so she fixed the food on a wood heating stove. Luckily, Simpsons had plenty of eggs and other food on their big farm. When Haskell and Lethia Cartwright sent their boys out to the highway to look for stuck motorists that same morning, they came back down the lane with twenty-one desperate people.

After the 1950 blizzard, as if Vernon wasn't enough of a circus, here comes Ernest Ross driving his farm tractor across the cement bridge with Skyline Bill straddling the hood. Skyline was yelling and waving his walking stick around like a cowboy in a rodeo.

BLIZZARD OF 1950, *L. to R.*, THE "Y" AND THE CEMENT BRIDGE, RILEY AND MABEL BOWERLY'S HOUSE, AND WELKER'S LUNCH

LET'S
PLAY
BRIDGE!

Above:
RUTH
ENGLE

Above:
EDDIE KARST, *front,*
AND DONNIE ENGLE

Left:
SHEP AND DAVID HULSE

Right: LURA BENNETT AND FRIEND

Left: TOM BOWERLY

Above: FAYE ENGLE

Left: JOYCE WHITCOMB

241

WILKIE TAYLOR AND HELEN WALT

ELOISE "WEASEL" CLENDENNING; ENGLE'S BRIDGE AT RIGHT

THE RHYTHMS CHANGE

While the town rhythms didn't seem to change very much when the 1940s turned into the 1950s, our household rhythms did. Just take ironing, for example. Our mother, who used to stand and iron dress after dress, didn't iron *anything* anymore. She gave each of us girls our own clean clothes, then divided up the rest of the family ironing among us, too. She did still wash down in the back room of the store, using the same wringer washer that sang the repetitive notes played before Johnny the bellboy yelled, "Call for Phillip Mor-ris!"

No matter how long our mother's housedresses agitated in Rinso-White, or how much starch she put in them, or how tightly they squeezed through the wringer, or how long they waved in the breeze, we were still reminded of her hard work when we passed the hot iron under her sleeves. Thank goodness she didn't have any dreams of her own and didn't want to do anything but take care of us and Daddy.

Darning wasn't so bad. We girls just pulled socks over light bulbs, scrunched down in front of the radio in little chairs we'd outgrown, and listened to *The Shadow*, or *The Lux Radio Theater*. When I told this to a boy at school, who'd moved in from Ohio, he said, "I would never wear a darned sock." Well, La-De-Da.

Teddy and Joe Eddie probably would never have to darn or "arn" because they were boys. (We had to call Joe Eddie by both his names since Daddy had tried very hard to name two sons after all his friends, while sticking his own name in there, too. Teddy's name was Richard Theodore.)

Teddy was the feisty one who fought by kicking and screaming. If that didn't work, he had what amounted to a Rumpelstiltskin fit, like on the day he and Mary Lou were gathering eggs in the shed and she was grabbing them all. Teddy jumped up and down waving his arms and kicking and yelling, "I want an egg! I want an egg!" so she broke one on top of his head. He started screaming because he thought the stuff running down his face was his brains. He screamed so loudly he woke up baby Joe Eddie, who was sick and Mommy had just got him down for a nap. Mary Lou got a spanking.

Teddy liked to go down to the river with the Slagle brothers, where they'd flip rocks over and catch a bucket or two full of snakes. They would take these snakes to the deep, walled-in area behind Slagle's house, turn them loose, then see how many they could get back into the bucket. But Teddy's excitement when he got home didn't involve snakes at all. He'd talk a mile a minute about how they all went into Slagle's house afterwards and opened a can of sliced peaches. "We could eat as many as we wanted to. We didn't even have to count'em out."

Yes, we counted out those things at our house because we didn't have dessert every day. Mommy got down the golden ruler when there was a loaf cake to be cut so everybody's piece would be the same size. We fought over the legs on the chicken and the cherries in the fruit cocktail (but we didn't fight over the pork in the pork 'n' beans). Regular day-to-day eating wasn't so important, though. There were too many interesting things to do in the world and having to stop and eat was a darned nuisance.

I think my brothers got skinny because they didn't have time to eat. Joe Eddie lived outdoors. He was so crazy about nature we swore he could communicate with birds and animals. He could make them come right to him and kept the whole backyard full of caged wild things surrounded by gourd vines.

He had inherited his love of nature from both our parents, except our mother didn't get to go out *into* nature like our dad did. But she always had something going on in her sink window, such as a caterpillar in a jar with holes in the lid, or a boxful of warm sand with turtle eggs in it, or columbines Daddy had picked for her at Cherry Park.

Our mother was organized. While we were getting ready for school, she put lunch food in a row of paper sacks standing on the kitchen table with our names on them. She kept a bundle of envelopes high on the kitchen shelf with names written on them, too, like *telephone* and *electricity*. Every payday she put money in the envelopes.

On Sunday mornings, when we watched her sit on the side of the bed and pull on her stockings, we Spurlock girls wondered if we'd ever have legs as pretty as hers. Looking down at our knock-knees we knew we wouldn't. It seemed only fitting that she got to keep on wearing silk stockings during the war, seconds Ted Bennett brought down from Real Silk, his work place in Indianapolis.

Kempers moved into a house, so we got the two rooms Grandpa had built for them on the end of our place. Daddy cut a doorway between our front room and the lower hall, put in a couple of steps, and we had what he called the "girls' dormitory."

Dorothy and Mary Lou shared a room and Katie and I shared a room. Dorothy was a shallow breather and we could hear Mary Lou yell at her in the middle of the night, "Dorothy, breathe!"

DOROTHY AND MOM;
WHICH TWIN HAS THE TONI?

Down in the girls dormitory we had terrible nicknames for each other, with the printable ones being "Marshmallow Nose" and "Pig Ears." Sometimes my sisters called me "Queenie," like they thought I thought I was special. It didn't seem like a bad name, and yet, that was the name of the breeder female, to put it politely, in Daddy's beagle hound family.

Every night Dorothy sat at her dressing table with one hand on her radio dial, the other holding a curl in place, and a sunburst of bobby pins sticking out of her mouth. She just kept turning the dial because she thought she was missing something on another station. It drove you crazy to be in the same room because you never heard all of a song. Usually, she was trying to bring in some faraway station in Tennessee, looking for the Pee Wee King band from Louisville. Her whole room was a shrine in their honor.

Katie and I lay in bed at night just thinking of awful things to do to Dorothy and Mary Lou. If we discovered we were both in bed and our ceiling light was still on, we'd call Dorothy in under the pretext we wanted to tell her something. After we told her something, we would say, sweetly, "Will you turn off our light when you leave?" She'd jerk that string and the metal tip on the end would snap all the way to the ceiling.

We residents of the girls dormitory all had different ideas of what being rich meant. Dorothy said rich people were people who had living room furniture that matched. I said rich people had chrome dinettes in their kitchens instead of tables and chairs made of wood. To Katie, richness was a yard full of green grass. Mary Lou thought rich people were the ones with dining rooms and lace tablecloths.

Katie and I remained close throughout our childhoods. For home basketball games we went to the gym separately and each sat with her own friends, but after the game we waited for one another at the front doors and walked home together. Some nights—

    when the game had gone into double overtime
    and the hour was late
    and ice was forming around the edges of puddles
    and the moon was behind a cloud
    and we were being chased by Vaughn Monroe and the
        Ghost Riders in the Sky—

we *ran* home. We didn't even slow down at the Jackson house; their one-story row of windows was just a yellow blur.

One such night, though, we were so giddy, probably because we'd just won an exciting game, we dared the Ghost Riders in the Sky to catch us. Yipee-I-O! I ran all the way to where the sidewalk ended in front of our church, then jumped down to the street. I turned my ankle when I landed and it hurt so badly I couldn't move; I just crouched there crying in pain. "Well," Katie said, looking down at me with her hands on her hips, "do you want me to go wake up Daddy, or do you just want to stay there all night and freeze to death?"

I had to think about that a long time. Finally I let her go get him because I was sure my ankle was broke. In fact, I *hoped* my ankle was broke, but he didn't grumble too much when he carried me down the hill. The next day it was clear my ankle wasn't even sprained, but I was glad it had happened. Our Daddy hardly ever touched us after we got past the toddler stage, and here he had carried me down the hill like I was a princess.

Daddy had left the swing factory and gone to Shackleford's in North Vernon, where chrome parts were made for Chambers ranges. Shackleford's was then bought out by Filsons, who forged wrenches and other things under loud drop hammers. Filson's had a wonderful Christmas party in the Vernon gym one year for their employees and families. Dorothy was home from nurses' training, so we all got to go and each of us received a nice gift. Daddy seemed confused; he wanted to show off all his daughters, yet he didn't want the men he worked with to even look at us.

When I reached junior high school, Mommy cut off my braids while they were still braided and mailed them to Aunt Betty, who wanted some real hair for a China doll she'd bought. The $5 check she sent back was the first check I'd ever received, and the exact amount for taking to Nauer's Drugstore and buying a little Brownie camera I'd been looking at in the glass display case.

The world was getting modern. Toothpaste no longer came in those awful soft tin tubes that developed new holes anyplace they got bent. If you squeezed one that was half empty, you ended up with a white octopus in your hand. Daddy sold the still-drivable Maxwell. The $25 he got helped pay for a used gray Plymouth, a car so ordinary nobody asked to ride with us anymore.

J. W. Coombs parked his maroon and cream Monarch bicycle with the big tank, chrome spring shock, and luggage carrier when he started driving his dad's car. After he bought his own '46 Plymouth, he was the coolest guy in town. He drove around with a toothpick in his mouth, his elbow resting in the open window and his hand at the top. When he met anybody, he didn't wave; he just lifted his forefinger. If a Mack truck had run into the back of that Plymouth, he wouldn't have changed his expression. The toothpick might have wiggled slightly, but J. W. Coombs wouldn't have lost his cool.

In junior high school I wasn't making enough money babysitting, so I agreed to work in Grandpa's print shop, which looked a lot more fun than working in the store. It was a regular job, not a one-time deal of assembling printed papers or distributing flyers. Mostly I sat in front of open drawers full of little sections of type and set one character at a time, putting them in a composing stick, an adjustable steel tray in my left hand that held several lines. I laid heavy strips of lead between each line. Sometimes I ran the press, but he usually did that. He said it was such a mess to ink, but probably he was afraid I'd get my fingers under the roller.

The print shop, now in the basement of Cadby's Folly, had always been an advantage to us. When we played school—there were enough of us we didn't have to bring in outsiders—we had plenty of paper and used real report cards from Vernon School (that were just a little crooked). At Vernon school we got to flash printed basketball schedules even before the coaches had them.

After I learned to type in high school I earned some money also by working for Mr. Huelson, the county superintendent, because he didn't have a secretary. His office was still in the same place, but Eddie Rogers was running a bait shop where the wallpaper store had been.

Just after I started my senior year of high school, Mom shocked us all by getting out her black dress with the little skunks on it. Wait a minute, she only wears that when she's... I was very unhappy and said some terrible things to her. I told her we couldn't afford any more kids.

THE BAIT SHOP, JAKE'S FRONT PORCH, AND VANGORDEN'S

My embarrassment subsided somewhat when I discovered another girl in the senior class had a mother in the same condition.

By the first of February I was giving Mom a hard time again, because I would hurry home for lunch and she would still be there instead of at the Seymour hospital having that baby. Yes, it was going to be born in a hospital, so I wouldn't get to dress it, like Dorothy got to dress Joe Eddie after he was born. But I wanted to hold that baby and take it all over town and show it off. I wanted it to be a girl, and it was. Marcia Darlene Spurlock was the cutest little baby girl ever to come to Vernon, and I got to send the telegram to Dorothy and Aunt Betty.

Marcia waited over a year to get even with me for not wanting her to be born. She waited until the most tender, moving, reverent part of my wedding, then she let out a big, ugly belch.

About six weeks before that I had walked up to the print shop and set up my wedding invitations. Although I hadn't thrown type into that stick for several years, I still remembered where all the letters were in the drawer trays. I used Grandpa's fanciest type and sprinkled silver powder on the print before it was dry.

While addressing the invitations in my room, I heard Joe Eddie outside my door asking to come in. He was not quite six and thought of me as the oldest sister because Dorothy had left when he was only three. When I told him to come in, he threw back the curtain, burst into my room, and made this announcement: "Carol, I don't want you to get married."

I was shocked. "You're crazy about Don," I said. "Why don't you want me to marry him?"

"Because, he answered, "I want us all to stay together."

THE ONLY PICTURE TAKEN OF US "ALL TOGETHER"
Front: TED AND JOE.   *Back*: DOT, KATIE,
DADDY, MOM HOLDING MARCIA, ME, AND MARY LOU
(in her tomboy stage)

How the paths of a boy and a girl growing up in a town of 430 could cross so seldom defied logic. Maybe it was because Don Layman attended the Presbyterian Church and I attended the Baptist...yet our churches united for some activities. Maybe it was because he was earning money by taking care of yards all over his end of town from the time he could push a mower...but he did a few yards on our end of town, too.

All those years he ran around with Bert Ochs while I ran around with Charlona, we were never at their house or in their van at the same time. Surely he was with me in the crowd standing between the north curve and the Narries that winter night in 1952, watching the swing factory burn down. The only thing I noticed about him in grade school—he was a year ahead of me—was that he wore corduroy pants to school while the other boys wore jeans and overalls, and he was always playing mumblety-peg with his pocket knife.

So Donnie Layman was sixteen years old and beginning a weekend job at Shotgun's before I actually "met" him. I was staying over the hill at Aunt Vonda's that weekend and she sent me to the station for a carton of orange pop. (We often drank pop and played rummy after her kids went to bed.) I must have been one of Don's first customers because he had an awful time with the cash register when he rang up that orange pop. He was making all kinds of faces, and when he flashed those dark eyes and dimples, cupid shot that first tiny arrow into my heart.

At first I didn't know I'd been wounded. I didn't even realize it when I started looking for excuses to go to Grandpa's store when Don was running the station. Then I started finding myself at Shotgun's watching television shows I didn't like, just to get a whiff of that deadly, masculine mixture of gasoline and Vitalis. I would just happen to end up down there the way my mother used to just happen out her front door when Dick Spurlock was walking to the post office.

Don Layman not only had dimples, he had a bright red Cushman motor scooter with a chrome devil on the front fender thumbing its nose. What a rebel. He had built a special trailer to hook to the back of his Cushman so he could haul his lawn mower around town and do even more yards. He was saving money for his own car instead of his dad buying it for him. I liked that in a man.

When I did realize I'd fallen for Don Layman, who still didn't know I was alive, I got mad at him. I didn't wait all those years and get this close to dating age just so I could limit myself to one boy. When I turned sixteen I was going to date *every boy in Vernon High School*, then, during the October of my twenty-first year, when the whole town smelled of burning leaves, I was going to seriously fall in love. And, after years of using Carol Spurlock, the neuter friend, for sending messages to the popular girls, boys were starting to notice *me* , darn cute boys. When they found out

DON LAYMAN ON HIS CUSHMAN

I was turning them away for a boy who wouldn't even give me a second look, they called me a fool.

Forget the plan. By now my heart must have been quite visible on my sleeve because everybody in town was "helping" me, including the big girls. Whether I wanted to or not, I got to hear about every move Don Layman made.

I found some solace in the fact that the

252

guy hadn't dated anybody yet because he still preferred hunting and fishing...until a terrible thing happened. A blonde from Kentucky came to spend the summer with her aunt, who lived across the highway from Laymans, and I started seeing her with Don. When I teased him about it, he said he was being forced to entertain her.

One Friday evening at dusk, he was "forced" to take her down to the Commons on his Cushman. I think he wanted me to see her on that motor scooter with her hair blowing back, because he could have gone down Brown Street. But no, he had to whiz her off the highway right across from me.

Dorothy and her friends teased him about it at the station the next day and he said they'd gone to the Commons to hunt night crawlers. "Sure," I said when I got the report. "That's what a girl wears for hunting night crawlers—white tee shirt and shorts. That's what you wear to get down on all fours and slap your hand on those slimy worms before they can get back into their holes. I used to sell night crawlers and that's what I always wore to hunt them, white tee shirt and shorts!"

I saw them at the county fair together. They had just got off the Ferris wheel and Don was looking all over the ground for some change that had fallen out of his pockets. Ha Ha, I said. We were in the middle of the big polio scare and somebody had brought an iron lung to the fair. They'd hooked it up and put a microphone in front of it, I suppose to remind us not to swim in water with scum on it. So no matter what you did at the fair that year, or wherever you went at the fair, all you could hear was that rhythmic, labored, breathing sound, and I hoped it ruined the day for Don Layman and his blonde. Heck, she probably wasn't even a *real* blonde.

That awful, long, hot summer eventually ended, she went back to Kentucky and I never saw her again. I had a feeling, though, that Don Layman had elevated girls into a category a notch closer to hunting and fishing. *Finally*, he realized he'd been in love with me all along. Our blending was such a gradual thing there was no clear line between my riding home from someplace with him and our actually dating.

Daddy gave us girls lots of rules, and the only reason he needed for making up another one was "because I said so." He wouldn't let his daughters wear shorts anyplace but home, didn't let Dorothy go out for cheerleader because she might "show her pants" and would have to ride on a bus with boys, and wouldn't let us swim at the Commons. So I wasn't surprised when he shook his finger down at me and said, "I don't want to see you on the back of that motor scooter." I did ride on it a few times, but, in respect for his wishes, we rode down by Dryden's bridge and other places where he wouldn't have to look at me.

Don Layman and I weren't officially "going steady," but neither of us dated anybody else. Driving his dad's black 1948 Pontiac, which he had shined until it looked like an onyx, he picked me up on date nights exactly at 6:30. We'd be sitting in North Vernon's Park Theater when the movie started at 7:00.

He said he *wanted* to go steady with me, but he couldn't get his class ring off his finger. My friend Joyce took care of that on Halloween when the three of us were sitting in a drugstore booth and she happened to have some slivers of soap in her pocket. At school the next day, after wrapping layers and layers of adhesive tape around the band, I showed everybody that Don Layman had "given" me his class ring.

About this time my family started embarrassing me. Eight-year-old Teddy always had to comment on Don's promptness. "What do you do?" he asked Don one evening, "sit up in front of the church with your motor running till

6:29?" Daddy didn't help either, by saying more than once, "I know she's ready; she's been looking out the window for ten minutes."

My sisters were the worst. I came to regret those years Katie and I decorated the dress form and rolled it over to our window blind to make silhouettes when Dorothy was sitting out front with a boy. But that wasn't nearly as bad as what my sisters did to me those rare times when Don and I were alone in the front room sitting on the couch.

Their joke involved a certain...convenience in the girls' dormitory for the girls who didn't want to go to the outhouse in the middle of the night. A girl might be afraid of spiders, or the weather was so cold that by the time she sat on the icy outhouse seat she didn't have to go anymore, or maybe she hated the feeling of a slipper full of snow.

Whatever, anyone who ever slept in the same end of town with one of these conveniences was all too familiar with the sound of that noisy metal lid trying to find its place in the middle of the night, grinding all around the rim. That's what my sisters did; they clanged and ground that lid all over the place while Don and I were trying to get romantic on the couch. Sometimes I could even hear them giggling through the fingers pressed over their mouths.

Don, having indoor plumbing at his house, didn't know what the sound was and ignored it, but *I* sure knew what it was, and I always felt the top of my head getting hot. Of course, by the time he left and I went looking for my sisters, they were at their friends' houses, or sitting safely in a booth at the drugstore, sipping cherry Cokes, completely innocent.

After our movie dates, Don and I would park down the lane to Bluebell Island, or just stop at Ochs's barn at the beginning of the lane. Sometimes Ted Collins and Sue Armstrong would get there first, and we made a big production of getting around that '41 DeSoto while waving and

AT TUNNEL MILL

making faces at them. Ted *had* to park close to home; his parents checked the speedometer whenever he got back. One time he forgot to reconnect it after driving out to Sue's farm and got into trouble.

When Don and I were parked in the lane to Bluebell Island one night, we sealed our union by committing that most intimate act two Vernon kids could commit: We told each other about our treasure chests.

I told him first about my cigar box painted silver, with old ring sets and pieces of colored glass glued to the lid. It had contained, among other things, broken jewelry, rocks with gold on them, a penny mashed on the railroad track, sequins and seed beads off an old dress from the 1930s, and a picture of Jesus. I even told him what Rosanna Sandefur and Joyce had kept in their treasure box, including White Star ticket stubs they'd pick up at the drugstore corner.

Don's treasure had been too valuable to hide anyplace in town. He said he'd hid it out along the railroad track between the trestles. His treasure was in a coffee can and its most important contents were gold watch chains given to him by his grandpa Layman. But in spite of his hiding it so well, he went out there one day and it was gone.

I liked going to Layman's house. Don's dad still teased me, but he almost acted afraid of me, too. Why would a grown man be afraid of his son's sixteen-year-old girlfriend? I really scared him once, when Don and I were both in the basement after swimming in the river down behind their house. Harold Layman stepped into the basement's outside entrance just as I stepped out of the shower with a towel around me. As if his face wasn't white enough, I dropped the towel (and revealed that I still had my bathing suit on). During the rare times Don and I were in the house alone, they had us sit near the picture window so the neighbors could see that we were just watching television.

Don's mother, D'Ette, was a short woman with a very sweet voice. Like most mothers, she was always busy. When she wasn't doing housework, she was doing swing factory work. She went up there to the sewing room in the evenings sometimes.

Sandra Layman, Don's younger sister, was one of Vernon's prime pranksters. She ran around with a bunch of kids who shared a lot of laughs about our little town and had nicknames for everybody in it. When they got bored, one of them would say, "Let's go up to Hunt's and try on the shoe." Yet the little old ladies loved Sandra. Maggie Abbett would actually let Sandra come to her house every Halloween and go through her trunks of old clothes for costume material, this woman I couldn't even get a wave out of.

In all our years of dating, Don and I had only two fights, or rather, near-fights. One was his fault and the other was mine. He got into trouble for getting too fresh with me one evening when we had pulled off the road out by the dog farm bridge. "Take me home," I said, which he did. The next morning when I got up to get ready for school and raised my window blind, I squinted and batted my eyes, not believing what I saw. Don Layman was sitting outside about to freeze to death in his newly bought '41 Ford. I got dressed, went out and talked to him, he apologized, and we made up.

What I did to irritate him started off innocently enough. At least I thought so. I was babysitting up on the hill when Florence Collins came across the street and asked me how to make seven-minute frosting. Well, I was pretty flattered, what with a housewife asking me, a high school girl, how to cook something. I said, "I'm about through here; I'll be over."

The icing turned out to be for a birthday cake honoring Florence's son Albert, who was Don's age and flirted with me, sometimes right in front of Don. I fooled with that cake a lot longer than I'd planned to, and when I got home and ran down to Shotgun's to see Don, he wanted to know where I'd been. When I told him, he frowned and quit talking to me.

What a miserable evening, sitting on the curb at the store end of the building, waiting to talk to Don. I could have sat on the bench, where D.L. + C.S. was carved along with everybody else's initials, but sitting on the curb looked more pitiful. I hoped it looked as pitiful as freezing in a '41 Ford. Why did he have to be so busy? Every time a car pulled in he had to pump gas, wash the windshield, check the oil, check the water, check the antifreeze, put air in the tires, all that stuff. And cars pulled in one after another.

While I waited, I thought about all those times, when Don first came to work here, that I had primped an hour at my dresser before breezing past the station "on my way to the store," hoping he would be outside waiting on a customer and see me. But, *there were never any customers then.* Don would be inside someplace and probably didn't see me at all. Ignoring the puzzled look on Grandma's face, I would pass directly through the store, slam the back door, return to my room, study my profile, and pout.

This evening he was all customers. Hunkered on that curb in a drizzling rain, I barely could hear the filling station radio and Johnnie Ray singing "Cry," Rosemary Clooney singing "Half as Much," and Joni James singing "Why Don't

You Believe Me?" I did hear the train whistle blowing, first for the Grayford crossing, then the second trestle, then the first trestle. Suddenly I knew what the grownups meant when they said the loneliest sound in the world was that whistle blowing for the Grayford crossing on a rainy night. I would have been even bluer had I known it was about the last time I would be hearing that locomotive whistle; the diesels were coming.

To make matters worse, I hadn't told Don everything. I hadn't told him about his class ring. It was missing...buried, I was afraid, in Albert Collins's birthday cake. I kept picturing not only Don's reaction, but the Collins family, gathered around their party when somebody bit into that big chunk of metal and adhesive tape.

I was getting a stomachache.

When finally I had a chance to talk to Don, at *closing time*, we made up. I never did tell him about his ring, which had been a wise choice because I found it the next day, in the pocket of an apron hanging on a nail in the Spurlock kitchen.

L. to R. COURTHOUSE, DADDY, QUEENIE AND FAMILY, JOE SKINNER, AND JORDAN'S FUNERAL HOME

DONNIE AND RUTH ENGLE
GETTING HUGGED BY THEIR
MOTHER WHILE STINKY
STANDS BY

A 1951 SNOW

MARCIA WITH CADBY'S FOLLY IN BACKGROUND

BUDS THAT DIDN'T OPEN

Betty Evelyn Spurlock

None of us Spurlock kids knew our little sister, Betty Evelyn. I call her our little sister even though she was the firstborn, because she was just a baby when she died. She was what they called a "blue baby." They said her skin was a bluish color because of a heart defect that did something to her blood. Whenever we went to the cemetery to play, we always stopped to visit her grave.

Alice May Schnadinger

When we were in the second grade, Alice May Schnadinger, an apple-cheeked girl with pigtails, got sick. The teachers were making a fuss over her and some smart aleck girls in the class were jealous, so they started saying, "Call an ambulance," and things like that.

Alice May must have heard, because during the lunch hour Alice May's big sister cornered us and gave us a good talking to. We felt terrible and deserved to. As for me, I put the entire incident out of my mind as fast as I could, except to try to make up for it.

The following August it all rushed back into my face. Jordan's ambulance had left in a hurry and headed south, so we all lingered close to the highway to watch for it to come back through on its way to the Seymour hospital. But when Jordan's reached the bridge, they turned the siren off and slowed down. We supposed another old person had died. But it was Alice Mae Schnadinger who had died. Dr. Green said she had strep throat and her throat had swollen shut until she could no longer breathe.

Schnadingers lived off of State Road 7, where their handsome daddy started his school bus route every morning, but the viewing hours were held at their grandma's house on the highway. My mother wanted to go because she and Alice

JUANITA FITCH AND ALICE MAY
SCHNADINGER IN THE SCHOOL YARD

May's mother had been classmates at Vernon school, good friends, and she wanted to see her. She thought I should go, too, because Alice May had been my classmate.

We arrived at Schnadinger's all too soon. I didn't want to climb the steps to that house; I wanted to stay in the car with Daddy. But, of course, I couldn't. The coffin was completely open and Alice May looked like she was asleep. Her mommy was crying and said to my mommy, "Now I realize what you went through when you lost your baby."

I looked at Alice May a long time. When my gaze reached her shoes, I was startled. I had never seen shoes like these. They were clear; you could see her anklets right through them, the most beautiful shoes I had ever seen. I imagined Cinderella's slippers must have looked like Alice May's shoes. They were just made for dancing into Heaven, I thought, and I felt better when I went back down the front steps. But I knew I wouldn't forget Alice May Schnadinger for as long as I lived.

David Lee Kemper

My cousin David Lee's death was the most painful one that happened while I was still at home. I went to pieces

262

at Jordan's and didn't make it to the cemetery. He was only ten years old, and even though he'd had rheumatic fever for years, his death was a shock to us all. I think it hit me hard because I had spent lots of time with him, babysitting and staying with Vonda.

Dorothy said she remembered David Lee as the curly haired little boy pulling his red wagon to the store for groceries. He hardly got to go to school at all. His neighbor, Laura Hess, taught him at home.

D. C.'s mother was staying at the Kemper house when the phone call came from the hospital. Thinking she was doing the right thing by removing painful reminders, she hid everything that had belonged to David Lee before his parents got home. She put away the Christmas presents made by his sisters and already wrapped. When Vonda arrived, she went wild until she found everything.

TEDDY AND DAVID LEE

David Lee's death occurred during the year between my graduation and my marriage, when I was working at the rug factory in North Vernon. For many days afterward, I could see tears falling and disappearing into those rugs as I pushed them under that row of needles. The rugs weren't damaged; rich ladies who bought Regal rugs in New York department stores would never know there were tears in them.

Looking around with blurry eyes at all the women in front of all the whirring machines, I remembered unhappiness and grief each had shared while we sat on soft piles of rugs eating our lunches. I realized for the first time that a lot of rugs probably went out of there with tears in them, and many family gardens had grown buds that didn't open.

THE COLD WATER GIRL PICTURE HANGING
IN HARRIET McKINNEY'S HOUSE

THE FREE SHOW

On Monday evenings in the 1940s, we kept an eye on the summer sky behind Nellie's house. Other than a stormy county fair week, nothing was more devastating than a rainfall on Monday night. There would be no second chance on Tuesday; the big man with the dark, wavy hair would be showing his free show in another town. That's what everyone called the movie on the courthouse lawn, "the free show."

Before dark, Vernon boys helped the man unroll a huge white canvas and tie it between two walnut trees up near the courthouse, on the left side of the front walk. Down on the perimeter he would set up his projector under the streetlight in the middle of the block. He was tall, rather rounded, and always mopping his face with a white handkerchief. At dusk he played a dozen scratchy records, like a stationary Pied Piper, and people began gravitating toward the courtyard. They came to the tunes of "Smoke, Smoke That Cigarette," "My Happiness," and "Cool Water."

They came from the upstairs apartments across the street, lugging wooden chairs from their kitchen tables. From the more distant parts of Vernon they pulled their Radio Flyers, the entire family employed in balancing its towering load of folding stools and blankets. Once empty, the wagon itself would be used by the small children, who would sit in it swinging their feet through the first half of the movie and sleep in it the second. They came in wheelchairs, Hazel Sandefur always bringing her neighbor, Gertrude Holmes. People drove or walked miles from the country with their blanket rolls, army cots, and oak steamer chairs made at the swing factory. We got to see other kids' mothers that we never saw any other time.

Just as they had their regular places at Vernon's churches and basketball games, each family settled down in its own special spot. Also, as in the churches, most young people could sit anyplace they wanted to, as long as that place was in front of their parents. So they usually congregated on low-slung blankets up front. Sandra Layman would head for this area carrying a dishpan full of grapes for eating and throwing.

Teenaged boys, too tough to bring anything to sit on, sauntered around the periphery looking cool. Casper Clendenning, the town marshal, stood at the very back with arms folded across chest, feet spread apart, trying to determine which boys most likely had firecrackers in their pockets. With twilight still on hand, some of these boys scouted the front half of the crowd, each deciding which girl's blanket would be blessed with the presence of his little behind. He hoped for cool weather to justify snuggling the blanket around them. Some blankets were more popular than others, and many a heart was broken at the free show.

During the socializing before the movie, fragments of laughter and conversation wafted through the courtyard on maple breezes. Corn popping in front of Hunt's store sent its aroma across the street to work the crowd. About this time Jake Swarthout would come out onto his front porch and sit down on his glider, where he would spend the rest of the evening pretending *not* to be watching the movie.

Finally, the man with the sweaty brow—stranger, hero, now executioner—would put the black hood over the streetlight globe above the projector. Even as tall as he was, he used a stepladder. Maybe that's why his crumpled white shirt was always pulled half out of his trousers.

Children squirmed and giggled. Young housewives in print dresses, sitting with crossed ankles, clasped their hands in their laps and straightened their spines. The crowd stopped murmuring and poised itself for the show. We watched a cartoon first—the background music was always classical—then a short subject, often the Three Stooges, or Leon Erroll fighting with his wife, Dorothy.

Intermission time came at the end of the feature's first reel. There would be some stirring and stretching then, a few people strolling up to the courthouse to get drinks from the tin cup wired to the water pump. Up there you could see backwards the only color of the evening, some slides of the Vernon businesses that sponsored the movie. These slides were predominantly faded pink, faded yellow, or a combination of the two. Along about slide four or five came the inevitable gob of hair, or the dead bug, either of which brought spontaneous applause and whistling from the front of the audience. And the big man would mop sweat from his brow.

If a boy ever was to slip his arm across the shoulder of a girl, it would be during the second half of the movie, when its damsel was in her deepest distress. He would first decide if the thrill would be worth the razzing he would take the next day, and if she had a strict daddy. The daddies were back there all right. If you turned you could see their cigarettes glowing. (Of course, all wasn't perfect innocence. A few "bad" people in the town family necked right in front of everybody.)

The movies weren't Hollywood's best; there were a lot of cowboys and Canadian mounted police. A few scenes made lasting impressions though, such as the eagle carrying off the little girl, and there was a blonde named Marjorie Woodworth who enthralled young and old alike. No, the movies themselves weren't memorable.

What sticks in the mind for life is the picture of us all
laughing and crying together
on the courthouse lawn
watching the free show
on a midsummer night
in Vernon, Indiana.

END

267

A WEDDING IN VERNON   MAY 27, 1956

L. to R., KATIE, MARGARET REESE,
MOM, ME, AND DON

EPILOGUE

Uncle Shotgun died in 1965, three weeks after Grandma, as if he had pledged to stay around just long enough to take care of her. Surrounded by friends, he was laughing, probably holding a handful of trumps, when he simply slumped down in his chair at the Cherry Park campers' card table and was gone.

Mom and Dad bought Cadby's Folly, including the huge yard with real grass in it. No longer limited to a sink window, Mom planted things everywhere. Today people walk down from all over town to see her moonflowers vining and her primroses spinning.

She's too busy to do much babysitting with great-grandchildren. When the town elections are held every other March (thanks to Vernon's unique charter), she's "der inspector." She gets to come out and say, "Hear ye, hear ye, the polls are now open," sometimes in front of TV cameras.

Our daddy died of cancer in 1970 and was buried in the Vernon Cemetery, very close to Alice May Schnadinger. A mockingbird that surely had traveled the entire globe sang at his burial. Hanley Cartwright, a gifted musician, came up to me afterward and said in a somber voice, "Carol, I visited your daddy when he was dying. I went down to play some religious music for him on his piano, but all he wanted to hear was the "St. Louis Blues."

Mom cared for him at home almost to the end. When the call came from the Columbus hospital, all of us didn't get there in time. Mary Lou did, and started crying at his bedside. Although no longer able to speak, he pointed his finger toward the door. No emotional displays in front of Richard Spurlock, thank you. I drove as far as Scipio, where I met my family coming back toward Vernon.

We all get together once or twice a year, whenever Dorothy comes up from Florida, where she's a private duty registered nurse. Katie, still the adventurous one, has been married many happy years to a man she met through the personal ads. When she isn't traveling the world with him, she's working on her collection of Vernon photographs.

AT THE 1991 CADBY REUNION - *Front*: TED, MOM, AND JOE
Back: MARCIA ME, KATIE, MARY LOU, AND DOT

Mary Lou works in a grocery store at Westport, in the next county. She and her husband are restoring their huge Victorian house. Mary Lou can play every musical instrument imaginable. Ted is office manager and systems analyst for the Southeastern Indiana Telephone Co-op. He loves computers. Joe works at Cummins Engine Company in Columbus. He'd still rather be outdoors. Joe and his son are carrying on the tradition of the Cherry Park campers.

Marcia is a graphic artist at Indianapolis. She can design anything, including book jackets. I'm sure glad she was born.

After Nellie Stout died in 1959 and her property was put up for sale, our mother went across the street and got a start from her bleeding heart bush. It had blossomed every spring, for as long as we could remember, against the back of Nellie's house. Mom was afraid something would happen to the bush and it would be gone forever. She was right about the first part, but I took a start off my mother's bush and to this day the two of us have kept Nellie Stout's bleeding hearts blooming. (Raindrops on the leaves *still* look like quicksilver.)

Jake Swarthout seemed to stay around forever. He didn't make his goal of 100 years, but did reach well up into his nineties. My own daughter and son, in fact, got to witness his antics in the Vernon Baptist Church, prompting one of them to ask aloud a question adults were thinking to themselves. We were driving home one Sunday when the daughter asked in all the unvarnished candor of youth, "Mommy? Why doesn't Jake die?"
"Honey," I answered after some thought, "God is putting off Jake Swarthout as long as he can."

The Roseberry family took care of Harriet McKinney in her old age and she eventually died of shingles. For more than four decades I believed Harriet McKinney didn't like me and I believed I didn't like her. During the two years the chapters of this book floated around in my head I continued to believe that. It wasn't until I typed the very last line of her section—as an afterthought—that I realized just what she had done for me. I felt so guilty I cried. Then I picked a spray of blossoms off of Nellie Stout's bleeding heart bush, drove out to Cherry Park, and put them on Harriet McKinney's grave.

I even put one sprig on her brother Jake Swarthout's grave, which is about twenty feet away. It was the only grave in the whole family plot that already had flowers on it—fresh flowers—and I couldn't help but wonder who had put them there.

Some people said Harriet and Jake made up in their last years. Several even claim credit for a reconciliation, but I never saw any signs of it. I was more concerned about Prof Jackson dying an athiest. Unfortunately, I had already moved out of Vernon when Jake and Prof had their famous cane duel at the liar's bench on the southwest corner of the courtyard. I'll never know if they were fighting over some philosophical point, or just fighting over the bench.

After Prof Jackson died, then Phyllis, some of their belongings went to a friend and neighbor, Golda Heilman. Included was a journal Prof had kept from 1943 to 1954. A typical entry: "Berlin falls to the allies. Planted first planting of sweet corn." In 1947, when he wrote that he had been asked to surrender the choir leadership in the Presbyterian Church, he stated that he had been attending church and Sunday school for seventy-three years. He wrote that he had directed the choir in the Vernon Presbyterian Church for thirty of those years.

Clara Harlow, my Old Dutch Cleanser lady, has been dead for many, many years, but Mary Roberson Proctor still has dreams about her. She says she dreams she is trying to get to Clara Harlow's house to see if she has food and fuel.

Mr. Griessbach, under the watchful eye of the trestle people, lived to be ninety years old. When Norman came back for a visit, he took his son around town and showed him off. Never slackening his determination to be of no trouble to his neighbors, the old man built his own wooden coffin and began sleeping in it. "This way," he told Dan Patterson, "if you come down here some morning and find me dead, you can just take me out and bury me."

Eventually he was taken to a nursing home, where he quit eating because they didn't serve his kind of food. He was going downhill fast when Pattersons bought a used house trailer, put it next to their home, and moved him into it. Roxana Patterson fixed his food the way he liked it and he thrived, spending his last years happily on the hill by the trestle.

When he died, he was given a nice funeral and buried in a purchased coffin. His church bought a stone for his grave. Dan Patterson, who had also helped with the funeral expenses, found some lost money behind Mr. Griessbach's chest of drawers. He found exactly the same amount of money as he had spent.

Even today a stroller in the Vernon Cemetery might discover newly-picked flowers on the grave of Emil Otto Griessbach, born February 19, 1879, in Leipzig, Germany; buried May 6, 1969, in Vernon, Indiana.

Haskell Cartwright is gone. He died not long after he and Lethia celebrated their golden wedding anniversary. Then their oldest child, Margaret, a month older than I, lost a battle with cancer. Before she died, she showed me a scrapbook from her school teaching days, which began at Seymour, in the next county. She pointed out a picture of one of her second grade pupils, a boy named John Mellencamp who is now a famous musician and artist.

Lethia still runs the cemetery. I can't imagine it any other way. The cemetery is getting full though. When the area down toward Bluebell Island was plotted off recently, I said to Don, "Let's get our lot right where we used to park; that big oak tree is still there." He agreed. Then I said, "We'd better go down and talk to Lethia before Ted and Sue Collins beat us to it. I don't want the four of us spending eternity ramming our coffins against each other like bumper cars at the fair."

THE HASKELL CARTWRIGHT FAMILY IN 1987 - *Front*: TOM, CHARLES, HASKELL ("HACKIE"), AND VERNON
Back: MARGARET, MARTHA, LOIS, HASKELL, LETHIA, IDA, VIVIAN, MARY, AND JANICE

Tom Semon's law school experience paid off for Vernon in his later years, when he was credited with keeping the state from rerouting the highway through Vernon. They wanted to straighten it out much the same way I had feared it would do by itself. Either way would have wiped out half the buildings. People say Tom accomplished this not with any law skills he had learned, but because he had gone to college with the governor.

After Charles "Muggy" Hartwell got older, he lived in the Semon home until the widowed Flossie became ill. Then Fred and Mary Biehle moved him into their house. A few years later the deaths of Mr. and Mrs. Biehle came one right after the other, and Charles Hartwell was taken to a nursing home. He had lived there about a year when a Biehle daughter, Freda, went and got him and took him to her house in North Vernon. Every time something is going on in Vernon, I see him walking around and visiting with people he knows. He seems very happy.

Mr. Nauer moved into a retirement home about the time Don and I got married. Martha ran the drugstore for awhile. She put a fuel oil heater and a juke box in the "other side." We found out, mostly from Coombses, that Mr. Nauer had been a generous man. He often gave them the key to his house so they could watch his console color TV.

Charles and Opal Kirkham, by putting a lifter in their house and one on their station wagon, were able to care for Sharon at home until she was thirty-eight years old. Her speech became hard to understand because of the Marie's disease, and her hands didn't work very well. But her wheelchair table was always covered with simple handiwork to be sold or given as treasured gifts.

She not only remained in contact with her first family, she traveled with Charles and Opal all over the United States. Out west she met her idol, Frankie Avalon. A highlight of Sharon Kirkham's life was the surprise appearance of a picture of herself and Frankie Avalon in the 1960 *Movie Screen Yearbook.*

In the nursing home, she developed cancer. When the doctors told her that chemotherapy might cause her to lose her hair, she said, "No big deal; I did that before." She died in her fortieth year. The last time I visited her, after her mastectomy, she was still smiling.

Thanks to a man from the card room, we recently discovered why we had to take so many wild game gifts to

Amy Dixon. Daddy and some other guys once tipped over her outhouse, he said, door side down, and she was in it. She yelled, "Darn you Dick Spurlock!" or something similar to that. Daddy asked her how she knew he was out there and she shouted, "If there's trouble, you'll be there."

TED BENNETT AND DAD, FRIENDS FOR LIFE

Dale Cooper, as it turned out, had not spent World War II guarding Vernon. He was flying cargo planes to Paris, all over the world, even to Casablanca. Knowing how to fly about every plane involved in the war, he volunteered to fuel check the B-17 when pilots were dubious about crossing the oceans in them. To do this, he flew to Freeman Field at Seymour and in the process buzzed the courthouse and his mother's house at Cherry Park.

Our schoolhouse was demolished and the gym became a community center after Jennings County consolidated into one big high school, where our children fell in love with the children of our most bloodthirsty basketball rivals. Ah, Shakespeare. The POWs who ran down the bluff behind

Vernon School were never found, but we expect them to come out any day now and ask if the war is over yet.

Vernon had looked like a dying town in the 1960s. The rebuilt swing factory was struggling—passenger jets didn't create a great demand for oak steamer chairs—, most of the stores on Front Street were empty, and many of the old houses in a state of disrepair. Then Riley Whitcomb, ever a man of vision, came up with an idea. Instead of trying to compete with bigger towns for manufacturing jobs, he said, why don't we capitalize on Vernon's unique assets?

He and some others decided to make Vernon a mecca of history, art, antiques, and collectibles. Enlisting the help of the local art club, he put easels and paintings in the windows of the Front Street buildings, changing the pictures periodically. When he ran out of easels, he made more.

I believe Riley Whitcomb saved Vernon because many old buildings that would have been destroyed have been refurbished and now house antiques and crafts. In 1976 the entire town was placed on the National Register of Historic Places.

The courthouse was renovated again in 1987 and the clock the county couldn't afford 130 years earlier was installed in the tower. Even better than that, a carillon also was installed in the tower and it chimes every quarter hour. It plays a full song at noon and at 4:30 and 6:15 in the evening, plus thirty-six holiday songs during the Christmas season, and special requests for weddings.

Today Vernon is a year-round tourist attraction and Josie Rogers' house inside the middle curve is the Bed and Breakfast of Vernon. But her catalpa tree is no longer in the little triangle. Hollow in the center, it had to be cut down in 1989, having outlived her by twenty-one years. When I drove by that stump recently and saw a catalpa sprout growing out of it, I laughed and said, "Hang in there, Josie."

The dumps have all been cleaned up and the bridges replaced, but Engle's bridge is still Engle's bridge and Dryden's bridge is still Dryden's bridge. They're just two of many families who are hanging onto their Vernon claims forever. About the time the oldest generation is ready to go to the back bedroom, the next one is ready to come home and retire. Yes, hard as it is to believe, Vernonites have left town and have worked all over the world. They didn't all huddle against the little village like I did, but they do come back.

What was it Nat King Cole used to sing? "If I Had to Choose Just One Day..."

If I had to choose a single time to be in Vernon, I, too, would select a Sunday, a Sunday morning. I'd be standing in front of the Vernon Baptist Church, still tingling with the awareness I felt during silent prayer, when I heard the old pendulum clock telling me I was surrounded by a God and a hundred and fifty people who loved me.

It's April. The trees are still bare enough that I can see the town below. Only the willows down by the Commons are green. Somebody's on the trestle, beneath a small plane suspended over Patterson's house as if by a thread, droning lazily in a flawless sky.

I'd plan my day in Vernon. First I'd walk down the hill with my mother, then change clothes and go all over town—around the courthouse square, up onto the culvert, past all those familiar houses. I would chat with Mrs. Reese over her white picket fence. At the schoolyard I would sit in the shelter house. Maybe I would walk up to Muscatatuck Park and hide under the rock of ages. I would...

Wait a minute...I can still do all these things.

INDEX OF LOCAL PEOPLE